WHAT'S THE DEAL WITH...

Social Security for Women?

MARCIA MACDONALD MANTELL

RETHINK PRESS

First published in Great Britain in 2019 by Rethink Press (www.rethinkpress.com)

Cover image © Shutterstock | mareandmare/Lina Truman

Author portrait by Leise Jones Photography

For my incredible sister, Michele.

I so admire all you've accomplished on that crazy, curvy road of life. Here's to memories of our Pepper Green bedroom, that summer in Minneapolis, and our Midwest road trip.

I wish you an amazing retirement.

Disclaimer

This book is intended to be educational only. The information is based on the Social Security's rules and regulations publicly available in the Social Security Act and Amendments, and on Social Security's website, www.SSA.gov.

All Social Security claiming decisions are ultimately each individual's responsibility. However, the information included here may help you with your claiming decisions. Social Security has multiple components, including old age and survivor benefits, disability, and Medicare. This publication focuses only on old age and survivor retirement benefits.

It is strongly recommended that you seek the advice of financial professionals who have expertise in Social Security matters and with your tax advisor before claiming benefits.

Only the Social Security Administration (SSA) can provide actual benefit amounts. The examples used throughout this book are for illustration purposes only and should be considered rough ballpark numbers. Any errors are unintentional.

Use your own Social Security statement and the tools on www.SSA.gov to estimate your own retirement benefit.

Contents

Introduction

No book on Social Security for women would be complete without recognizing the profound contributions made by two incredible women who forever changed the face of retirement.

Frances Perkins was the key architect behind the original 1935 Social Security Act and subsequent 1939 Amendments. In the 1930s, women did not have a place in government or political power. Yet, Frances, a staunch champion for women, was appointed by Franklin D. Roosevelt to be his Secretary of Labor. She was the first woman to sit on a Presidential Cabinet. One of her first orders of business when she arrived in Washington was to draft the Social Security Act. Then, she worked to add provisions for a social safety net for all women: workers, at-home wives and mothers, and widows in their retirement years.

Before she was the "Notorious RBG", Ruth Bader Ginsburg pushed the Social Security law into modern times. An original provision in the survivor benefits of the Social Security Act was designed to protect widows who were raising young children. They would receive a survivor's income benefit after the loss of the male breadwinner. Yet, when a man stayed home to raise his child after the death of his wife, there were no equal provisions. Mrs. Ginsburg's argument before the Supreme Court in 1975[1] changed all that. Her challenge of the traditional male-as-breadwinner/ female-as-homemaker model changed how government benefits are allocated. Consequently, women's earnings, while generally lower than a man's, were considered equal dollar for dollar.

It is with gratitude and great appreciation that all American women benefit from the efforts of these two women. They didn't start out as heroes, but they rose to the challenges of their day to ensure women of future generations could rely on a level of financial support and dignity in retirement.

---

1   Caspar Weinberger, Secretary of Health, Education, and Welfare *v.* Stephen Wiesenfeld; 420 U.S. 636; 95 S. Ct. 1225; 43 L. Ed. 2d 514; 1975 U.S. LEXIS 48.

Social Security: the bedrock of the American woman's retirement

Most books about Social Security focus on the nitty-gritty of its rules and benefits calculations, but fail to address specific questions women are asking:

- How much money will I actually get from Social Security?

- What are my options for claiming?

- How soon can I retire and start collecting my Social Security?

- Do I really get benefits on my spouse/ex-spouse?

When you have a specific question about your real benefits, knowing how to calculate your Average Indexed Monthly Earnings, or AIME (pronounced like the name "Amy"), or Primary Insurance Amount, known as PIA in Social Security lingo, just doesn't cut it.

Many Baby Boomer women and those in the younger generations are no longer dependent on their husbands for retirement income. They've built careers, control household assets, and are calling the shots for retirement. Yet they don't realize the power of Social Security and the important role it will play in their foundation for financial security in old age. Very few understand how they personally can fully benefit from this social insurance program.

Giving women the information they need

Getting ready to retire and leave that paycheck behind takes time and planning. The first step is to build a comprehensive retirement income plan. The second step is to consider how Social Security will become a key source of income throughout your retirement.

Getting good, practical information about Social Security helps you make good decisions about how and when you'll claim. There are consequences to your decisions that will last a lifetime.

All of this begs the question: What's the deal with Social Security for women?

In short, that's what this book is going to help answer.

From my travels around the country talking to women about getting ready for retirement, I know there are lots of mistakes made and lots of misperceptions swirling out there. Women don't yet understand the power of the program. Frankly, we've either been too busy to sit down and figure out how Social Security is going to work for us or we didn't know we needed to know.

Now you know. No more excuses.

How this book is organized

There are three parts to this book:

1. **General information about Social Security**. You'll read about how the program works, what information you need to know before deciding when to claim your benefit, and what the implications are for your retirement income.

2. **Social Security's four claiming categories.** Social Security considers you married, divorced, widowed, or single. The rules are different in each category. Jump to the category that applies to you. Read about how your benefit will be determined, and about real women who are in similar situations to yours.

3. **Other important information.** Social Security benefits have special characteristics and rules. You'll get an overview of other factors to consider such as taxes and what happens when you claim and keep working.

Each scenario in Part 2 comes from real questions I've received from real women all over the country. In most cases, the names have been changed to protect the innocent.

A special note for men

One last note: Social Security rules are the same for men. Your husband or brother or male friends can also read this book. To bring some simplicity to this complex social insurance program, the perspective and examples here are from women and about women.

The reasons I focus on women are two-fold:

1. I am a woman, so I feel I can speak about women's issues from the inside out.

2. Women who talk to me after presentations and events really want to understand their benefits. They didn't realize they had decisions to make about Social Security. They didn't understand that the decisions they make in their early 60s will impact their very financial security in their 80s and 90s.

It's all important. And there is no better time than now to get your head around this incredibly important program we call Social Security.

Where to get more information

There is so much important information about Social Security that it could fill 1,000 pages. Rather than reading all that, read the parts of this book that apply to you, then find more information on my blog, *Boomer*

Retirement Briefs, at https://boomerretirementbriefs. com. There you'll find:

- Free action plans and checklists for preparing for your Social Security benefit

- Worksheets for retirement planning

- More scenarios featuring women and how they are thinking about Social Security

PART ONE

SOCIAL SECURITY BASICS: FROM A BIT OF HISTORY TO HOW YOUR BENEFITS ARE CALCULATED

1
Women And Social Security – An Important Partnership

Each generation of women makes significant contributions to the generations of women who follow. Their sacrifices open doors for their daughters and granddaughters. For the past 100 years, women have increasingly worked outside the home, building careers and bringing home paychecks. As of 2018, 54% of women are the primary breadwinners in their households.[2]

With current paychecks come future Social Security benefits. When a person qualifies for Social Security on their own work record, they are considered "fully insured" for retirement benefits. Time was when most

---

2   Prudential (2018) *The Cut: Exploring Financial Wellness within Diverse Populations: 2018 Financial Wellness Census*. Newark, NJ: Prudential / StateofUS, pp 14–15.

women were solely reliant on their husbands for financial security in retirement. Today, women have just about caught up with men in being eligible for their own, independent Social Security retirement benefits.

In fact, the percentage of women who are now fully insured on their own merits has skyrocketed from 63% in 1970 to 86% in 2017. In comparison, 90% of men qualified as fully insured in 2017.[3]

This means that more women than ever have worked long enough and earned enough in wages or self-employment income to qualify for their own retirement benefits from Social Security. This is indeed an important step forward in women's financial journeys.

Women's Social Security benefits are critically important

Social Security becomes the foundation of retirement income for almost every woman in America. For women who have fallen on hard times, or didn't have a high-paying job, or didn't have the opportunity to build a large nest egg, Social Security does exactly what it was designed to do: keep older Americans out of poverty during their retirement years.

---

3   Social Security Administration (2018) Fast Facts and Figures About Social Security, 2018. https://SSA.gov/policy/docs/chartbooks/fast_facts/index.html

A staggering fact from the Social Security Administration states that, "46% of all elderly unmarried females receiving Social Security benefits relied on Social Security for 90% or more of their income."[4]

Retirement is not always the rosy dream we had hoped for. Having as much Social Security income as possible therefore becomes a critical factor for many women.

The first Social Security payment

The first person to receive Social Security benefits was a woman. She's become quite famous in the annals of Social Security history. Ida May Fuller was a legal secretary in Vermont. Her employer paid in a total of $24.75 toward her Social Security benefits. Her first check, dated January 31, 1940, was for $22.54. How long did she receive payments? For every month that she lived in retirement – in her case, until age 100. She died in 1975 after she collected a total of $22,888.92 in Social Security benefits.[5]

Ida May's story illustrates one of the most important features of Social Security: it provides monthly income every month of your retirement.

4   Social Security Administration (2018) Fact Sheet: *Social Security Is Important to Women.* https://SSA.gov/news/press/factsheets/ss-customer/women-ret.pdf (data is for 2016).
5   Social Security Administration, Historian's Office.

Shock and unhappiness

There is nothing quite like seeing the shocked looks I get when giving a presentation on Social Security. The first question I ask audiences who are age 50 and older is, "How much, on average, do Social Security recipients get in retirement benefits each year?" The answers from audiences range from $15,000 to $50,000 per year. In other words, very few have any idea of the real amount.

When I reveal the answers, the audience audibly gasps. In 2019, the average yearly payment for men was about $19,000, but for women it was about $15,000. That translates to about $1,580 per month for men and only $1,250 for women. There is outrage among the women. And often, one or more will shout "Why?" in disbelief.

Why women have lower Social Security payments

Why, indeed. When you think about your own life's path, you may recall some years when you stayed home to raise your children, or to take care of an aging parent or relative. You may have worked in part-time jobs or lower-paying jobs. Maybe it took you 20 years to climb the ladder, or you decided to go for a Ph.D. that took five or six years out of earnings. Whatever your personal path, most women find that it was not a straight line. With all the demanding roles we have to play, we often don't have a continuous career where our income increased consistently every year. It was more of a curvaceous path.

It turns out, however, that your wage history and your particular path greatly impact your Social Security payments decades later. You may find it surprising that Social Security is designed to be fair. It just doesn't seem fair when you compare his benefits against hers in many cases. One reason many women feel cheated is that none of us knew the rules of Social Security and how our benefits would be calculated when we started out on our work journey. And, really, why would anyone be thinking about Social Security benefits in their 20s, 30s, or 40s? After all, we're busy building a life, a career, and often a family in those earlier years.

Understand key aspects of the program

Let's put Social Security in perspective and focus on a number of key aspects of the program. It is, and always has been, a social insurance program. It was important to the architects of this program that it not be a welfare program. Social Security would be a benefit that each American could qualify for based on their own personal work and earnings history.

From the beginning, it was also recognized that women were key contributors to the economic success of a household. Running the home and raising the children had real value even though women didn't earn paid wages while doing this work. At the point of retirement, a woman's household contributions were nonetheless recognized and she was entitled to her own Social Security check. She would be eligible for up to half of her spouse's full retirement benefit. (We might argue here that at-home moms should be getting twice their husbands' benefits, but the formula doesn't work that way!)

The benefit formula for retirement is based on each worker's highest 35 years of average earnings. Your actual Social Security payment amount is, therefore, based directly on your real work history. In the case of so many women, our work history has been up and down, down and up. That's why, on average, women end up with a smaller monthly payment. We simply haven't worked long enough or earned as much income. Yet.

You can still influence your Social Security payment

If you are still quite a few years away from retiring, you may be able to improve your benefit amount. This happens if you keep working and earning more each year. If you are on the cusp of retirement, your benefit is pretty much final.

You'll want to take a look at your most current and up-to-date benefit estimate. You'll find that on your own Social Security statement. To access to your statement, and to help protect your Social Security number from cyber trolls and other bad apples and hackers, it's very important to set up your account at Social Security's website. Look for the icon "*my* Social Security" on the homepage or use the direct URL: www.SSA.gov/myaccount. It only takes a few minutes to set up your account.

Once you have your statement, take a look at your own work history. How many years of earnings do you have as of today? What is your estimated benefit amount when you retire?

You can make some decisions about how much longer you want to work based on what you see on your statement. It might make sense to keep working; your benefit could be increased substantially. You might decide that your work history is good enough and now you know how much to plan for in retirement. Or you may qualify for higher benefits based on your spouse's record. The point is, your statement is an excellent tool for helping you make decisions.

The moment of truth

Often times, attending a Social Security presentation is the first time that almost-retired folks face the reality of what it means to create retirement income. It is surprising to see that you are not going to get a heck of a lot of income from Social Security. And if you're a woman, on average you get a heck of a lot less. Call it a moment of truth.

Whether Social Security is going to be a significant amount of your retirement paycheck or not, it is a terrific program for older Americans. It is a social safety net that is critical to most retirees and their families. For the past 85 years and counting, Social Security has been the bedrock of Americans' retirement security.

It is not, and never was, intended to be a replacement for your employer's wages. It was, however, designed to keep some of our most vulnerable citizens out of poverty, and to provide each worker and their spouse with a modest income throughout retirement.

2
A Bit Of History

Let's go back to the Great Depression, which lasted from 1929 through the 1930s. America was at one of its lowest economic points, and our citizens were suffering mightily. There was little work to be had. Farms were unproductive after years of drought. If you had any savings, they likely disappeared with the crash of the financial and banking system. It was all but impossible to put a roof over your family's head. To say it was a bleak time and Americans were in dire straits is an understatement.

Years before the Great Depression hit, Congress had been discussing and debating whether there was a need to introduce a social insurance program to help impoverished elderly citizens. America had swung from an agriculture-based country to an industrialized country and the family-centric culture had been displaced by a more individual one. Thus, the elderly who had previously been cared for by younger family members in an extended family arrangement found themselves old and alone.

The sudden crash of the market and the severity of the Great Depression glaringly exposed the crisis of the aged. Many had lost their pensions and no longer had family to rely on.

The Social Security Act becomes law of the land

In a move championed by President Franklin D. Roosevelt, Congress passed the Social Security Act of 1935. Its specific goal was to provide retired workers with a modest foundation of income in retirement. Behind the scenes, one woman worked tirelessly to make Social Security happen: Frances Perkins, FDR's Labor Secretary. She was the first woman in a Presidential Cabinet and a staunch supporter of fair wage laws and protections for women and children.

From the very beginning, it was clear that Social Security was not a welfare program. Hard-working, fiercely independent American workers were not interested in a handout. Unless and until you qualify, you will not receive retirement payments. It was designed as a "pay-to-play" system.

And, to ensure that future recipients paid into the program, Congress placed the burden of making the tax payments on employers. There was to be no getting around the system if you worked for an employer. Protecting older and retired workers was critically important, and everyone was going to ante up.

A very different attitude today

Here's something that may seem unbelievable: In the early years, the Social Security Administration had to run marketing campaigns to encourage workers to get a Social Security number and apply for benefits. It was a significant effort to educate the population and to change the culture.

Today, it's quite a different story. People can't believe they have to wait until their 60s to claim their benefit, let alone understand that it is much better to wait until at least their Full Retirement Age (from ages 66 to 67) or until age 70 before they claim.

Many near-retirees are highly skeptical that the program will be there for them. They feel Social Security is an entitlement and they want to "get what's mine". They know the earliest age at which they can claim Social Security retirement benefits is 62, yet they don't know their own Full Retirement Age. They don't know that they will take a dramatic cut in benefits if they claim as early as 62. They simply want to "grab and go". For women, this is often the worst financial decision they can make. They lock in the absolute smallest amount of money they will receive from Social Security. And that may well become their most important income in old age.

Social Security is still critically important – 85 years later

To say that this program is important today does not do it justice. Virtually every American adult is keenly aware they will be receiving a Social Security payment and they count down the days until they can claim. It is an incredibly important part of every woman's household income in retirement.

As much as people complain about Social Security today, everyone wants their share. It is a gigantic program that gets bigger and more important every year. There are some 76 million Baby Boomers either claiming Social Security retirement benefits or on the verge of claiming. Another 65 million Gen Xers are nipping at the Boomers' heels. After 85 years, most citizens have become reliant on setting up their retirement years based on receiving Social Security.

Take a look at the level of support this program provides today:[6]

---

6   SSA Historian's Office; Social Security Fact Sheet for December 2018.

- In 2019, about 64 million Americans will receive over $1 trillion in Social Security benefits

  - 44 million are retired workers
  - 6 million are survivors
  - 14 million disabled persons, spouses, and dependents

- 5.5 million people were newly awarded Social Security benefits in 2017

- 55% of adult Social Security beneficiaries in 2017 were women

3
The Elephant In The Room

Before we dive in to more details about planning for your Social Security retirement benefit, let's address the elephant in the room. Many people are understandably concerned about the Social Security program and wonder (and doubt) if it will continue to be around. It is wise to question the viability of this program, but it is even more important to get the facts. The media hype and hoopla is a problem. The sensational headlines would stop anyone in their tracks. But rarely are there enough facts presented to help us understand the real situation. Let's get to the bottom of it all:[7]

---

7   The 2019 Annual Report of the Board of Trustees of the Federal Old-Age and Survivors Insurance and Federal Disability Insurance Trust Funds.

- The Social Security Administration forecasts the program will be here for the long haul. Their projections look forward 50 and 75 years at a time.

- Current funding by workers via Federal Insurance Contributions Act (FICA) taxes supports payments to the current retirees.

- The trust fund that underpins that program was tapped for the first time since the 1980s in 2018.

- Beneficiaries will continue to receive payments after 2034, but they could be reduced if Congress does nothing to shore up the system.

- If you won't be old enough to claim by 2034, you'll still apply for benefits, but they could be reduced from the estimates you currently see on your statements.

- The current estimates show that payments would be about 25% less for everyone after 2034.

The big message here is that Social Security will continue for more years than you will be alive. So long as you otherwise qualify for retirement benefits, you will get them. They will still be based on your personal work history; however, they will be reduced if Congress fails to take strategic and specific action.

Time to get in the game

What are the most important things all of us Baby Boomers, Gen Xers, and Millennials can do to stay on top of Social Security's solvency? There are many ways to get involved and stay involved, including these three recommendations:

1. **Get to know your representatives and senators**. Write to them. Talk to them. Join the AARP lobby group to keep pressure on Congress to do the right things to shore up Social Security. Each of our voices is important. Collectively pressuring our legislators can move the needle. As we all march closer to retirement, we may also have to march on Washington. Lace up your sneakers and get ready to act!

2. **Understand that the Social Security Act is a law.** It can only be changed by an act of Congress. (I guess that's better than needing an act of God, but sometimes it seems to be on the same order of magnitude.) The last major overhaul of Social Security was during President Reagan's administration in 1983. That's the last time the funding and solvency of Social Security's trust fund was threatened. The changes Congress made back in 1983 provided security until 2034, shoring up the program for 50 years. Surely our Congress can propose solutions for Social Security's current challenges to continue its health for the next 50 years.

3. **Get the facts, ma'am.** Don't let the headlines cause you alarm. Go to primary resources to get your facts. See what individual representatives and senators are proposing. See what Social Security is recommending. Get your facts from the horse's mouth. The best page on Social Security's website for these facts is www.SSA.gov/OACT/ solvency. Here you'll find the most recent proposals about Social Security solvency swirling through the legislative process. Stay on top of what your representative is supporting (or not) and make sure you let them hear from you. On a topic as important as our income in retirement, every single voice and vote counts.

In two of my 2018 *Boomer Retirement Briefs* blog posts, I wrote about this very issue of Social Security solvency. You can read them (and many other posts) at https:// boomerretirementbriefs.com.

4

The Most Important Document: Your Social Security Statement

It's easy to find out if you are eligible for Social Security retirement benefits and how much you may receive in retirement by taking a look at your most recent statement. And, it's truly important that you sign up today on Social Security's website to access your account – called "*my* Social Security". In fact, I think it is so important that you take this step, I'm going to encourage you to put this book down for five minutes, grab your cell phone or log in to your computer, and go to www.SSA.gov/myaccount to open your account. It is fast, easy, and essential.

What's in a statement?

Take a close look at your statement. It's a trip down memory lane. When you see 1979 as the first year you worked and earned that whopping $125, you'll scarcely believe it was that long ago that you worked at McDonald's or Burger King, Woolworths or JCPenney. You will want to make sure all of your personal information on your statement is correct:

- **Your name.** I know it seems obvious, but with marriages, divorces, remarriages, etc. it is easy to miss updating your Social Security records to reflect your current legal name.

- **Your date of birth.** Check to make sure there are no typos in your full date of birth – the right year, with the right month and day, and that the day is not off by one digit.

- **Your work history.** The IRS and Social Security share work and payroll/wages information. Today, things are automated and seamless, but back in the 1970s, 1980s, and 1990s, the process to "upload" your data was more manual.

Oh no – there's a mistake on my record!

What if you find a mistake on your Social Security statement? Well, it's up to you to get it corrected.

Updating your name or date of birth is a matter of providing original proof documents such as your birth certificate, passport, marriage license, or divorce decree and applying for a new Social Security card.

Where it gets harder is correcting your wage history. If you catch the error within the first year or two, you can call the SSA and request a correction. Technically, you have precisely three years, three months, and 15 days to correct wage data. (And, no, I didn't make up that rule.)

If you find errors from years or decades ago, Social Security has no obligation to update that information – you've missed your window. However, if you can produce original W-2s or your original tax returns, you can submit them and request a correction. There is no guarantee of success, but you can give it a try.

Before you deep-dive into those musty boxes in the basement or cobweb-covered piles in the attic, make sure you need to make that grand effort. If the missing year was likely a low-earning year, and it wouldn't be included in your highest 35 years of earnings for the calculation anyway, don't bother. However, if it was a high-earning year that would replace a $0 year, and you know you have original documents and you will feel better if you submit them, go ahead and make the effort.

A few things to note about your Social Security earnings record:

- **Some wages appear to be missing.** If you are a high-earner, you'll note that not all of your wages are shown in the "Social Security Earnings" column. They've been capped at the annual taxable wage base (TWB). This is the amount of your income subject to Social Security taxes.

- **Some years may contain zeroes.** Over a 40-year history, you may see periods where you didn't have any earned income. From staying at home raising your children to spending years in graduate school, it is common for women to have zeroes in their work record. Or, if you worked for an "uncovered employer" (see more in Chapter 5) you were not paying into the Social Security system – more zeroes.

- **Unemployment is not income.** Many people have been laid off during periods of their careers and could collect unemployment. "Unemployment" is technically insurance, and therefore not wages. Social Security is only collected on wage income.

- **Disability insurance doesn't count as income.** For moms, you may notice a big dip in your income the years your babies were born. That's because "maternity leave" falls under the disability insurance rules. Again, it's not considered income.

The big message here is: don't panic if you see some gaps and zeroes. Your first thought will probably be that your Social Security statement is wrong. It probably isn't. It's just that you've done lots of different things over the past 40, 45, or 50 years. Not all of them were paid jobs.

A note about the taxable wage base

Your statement reports your earned income each year, including any zeroes, up to the taxable wage base. The taxable wage base is a specific income amount where FICA taxes are capped. It changes every year. For example, in 2019 the taxable wage base was $132,900. If you earn less than that, you'll see all your earnings for 2019. If you earned more, you'll see your Social Security wages stop at $132,900. Your Social Security taxes are paid based on your income. Once you exceed the taxable wage base, no further Social Security taxes are due for that year.

Take a look at your wage history. If you know you made more than is listed on your statement, it probably means your FICA taxes were capped at the TWB.

Social Security's magic number: 35

When looking at your statement, the first thing you want to see is whether you already have 35 years of earnings. That's the magic number for Social Security. Social Security will select the highest 35 years available from your work history to calculate your retirement benefit.

Depending on your current age and the number of years you've been working, you'll see varying data on your statement. Your estimated benefits will be based on this information. Where do you stand today?

- **If you have 35 years or more of work history earnings:** You show dollars in at least 35 years since the first year you posted earnings. If you've stopped working, Social Security has your final data to run your calculations. If you continue to work, your new wages will be added to your work history each year.

- **If you have between 10 and 34 years of work history:** You either have years of work to come, or you have completed your career. Assuming you've completed work, Social Security will use your real information to calculate your retirement benefit. The calculation will include zeroes in your highest 35 years of history. If you stayed home for 10 years raising your children and worked for 25 years, you've got 35 years to work with. It's just that 10 of the years will be included with zeroes.

- **If you have between one and 10 years of work history:** You have not yet qualified for your own benefit. You may be able to receive a benefit as a spouse or ex-spouse or surviving spouse.

- **If you have no years of work history:** There are several situations where you may find that you have an entire statement filled with zeroes. These include the following (although this list is not necessarily exhaustive):

  - You worked for an "uncovered" employer who did not have to pay into the Social Security system. You'll receive a state pension instead.

  - You worked for a union that opted out of Social Security. In these situations, you'll receive a pension rather than Social Security in retirement.

  - You worked for the railroad. There is a separate retirement program that the railroad put in place about the same time Social Security got started. Railroad workers get a pension instead of Social Security.

  - You were married and did not need to work outside the home. Your statement will show a series of zeroes, but you will qualify for benefits as a spouse, ex-spouse, or surviving spouse.

Key points regarding your statement

Keep in mind when looking at your statement that your situation will be unique. Your career may have lots of twists and turns, or you might have spent 47 years with the same employer. Use the statement to see your own situation.

Social Security is going to use 35 years of your earnings as a key ingredient in your benefit calculation. You may have exceptions that result in reduced benefits or no benefits from Social Security at all. We'll look more specifically at some of these situations in later chapters.

Use your statement to make "work versus retirement" decisions. If you have 10 zeroes and you're 55 years old, should you work another 10 years? How much of a difference will it make to your monthly income? You'll have to run the numbers using the calculators on www.SSA.gov to see the real impact on your benefit or work with a financial advisor who has expertise in Social Security. Realize that each year of wages is only $\frac{1}{35}$ of your benefit calculation, so the result may not be what you expect.

A married woman's dilemma and disappointment

Married or formerly married women are often dismayed when they learn they don't qualify on their own work records for Social Security income. They want to know, now, at age 58, if they should try to find a job and work for the next six or seven years.

My answer is always a question: "Do you *want to* work outside the home?" Almost every time, their answer is "No." They face this dilemma of feeling disappointed and discouraged that they don't get any of their own Social Security, but they don't want to go to work. It stings less when they learn that they will indeed get their own Social Security checks. The amount will be based on the work record of their spouse or ex-spouse.

A related question has to do with the zeroes. Women who have 30 years of work and wages and want to retire now with their partners ask if they should just stick with the job and keep working until they reach 35 years of earnings.

My answer here is always the same: Run the numbers! Use the calculators at www.SSA.gov to see how much of a difference it will make to your monthly income if you work for another four or five years. These women clearly want to join their retiring husbands or wives and start their retirement lives together with them. So, why continue to work if you can afford to leave the job? The challenge becomes how to set up a bridge strategy until Full Retirement Age, which is the optimal time to claim retirement benefits.

Meet Michele: using her Social Security statement helped with career decisions

So many women's journeys have been filled with twists and turns. In Michele's case, she was married, then separated, then divorced. She has two daughters, whom she treasures. They are grown, college-educated, and starting their own careers, but getting them to adulthood was riddled with challenges and interesting opportunities. In the early years, her husband worked the "B" shift from 3:00–11:00 p.m. while she worked part-time from 8:00 a.m.–2:00 p.m. That way the girls were raised by both Mom and Dad.

Then, they had an opportunity to move to Asia for 2½ years with his job. It was an exciting adventure and Michele was happy to give up her job for such an incredible opportunity for her family. After a year abroad, she did get a job in Tokyo, but it didn't come with any contributions toward Social Security.

Going solo

Then, 15 years into the marriage, the relationship had run its course, and Michele and her husband split up. Michele became a single parent. She successfully ushered her girls through their high school and college years while working in a middle management job in a company that was struggling. Wages didn't increase over many of those years and promotions were delayed year after year. Relocation wasn't an option at that time, and the local job market did not hold many alternatives.

She managed to hold it all together with grace and good humor. She stuck to a budget, launched her girls, and found time to volunteer at her church and in networking groups. She even picked up a part-time job at a cooking store after her younger daughter went to college. It wasn't so much for the money, but the income didn't hurt. It was a way to explore future opportunities, meet more people, and get great discounts on her favorite cooking supplies.

A surprise 50th birthday gift

On her 50th birthday, Michele received a surprise "early retirement package" offer from her long-time employer. In fact, the offer came along with her 25th anniversary gift at the company. Yes, there were certainly twists and turns on her journey.

She jumped at the chance to find a new direction in her career. There would be no early retirement for her. What kinds of jobs would she want to pursue? Would this new job need to be higher paying, or could she start to scale back or go part-time?

Using her Social Security statement as a decision-making tool

One tool Michele used during the evaluation was her Social Security statement. What she saw in terms of her estimated benefits did not make her do the happy dance. At age 50, Michele only had 32 years of earnings under her belt. So close to the magic number... and yet so far. She saw that many of those years were from high school and college – part-time, minimum-wage jobs. Then, there were the early career years, followed by part-time work while she was raising her girls. There were three years of zeroes while living in Asia, but her last 10 years were looking pretty good.

Furthermore, while she meets the rules as an ex-spouse, and might be able to claim a higher benefit on her ex's record, she was, in fact, the higher earner. So, Michele's highest Social Security benefit will be from her own work record. She's not looking to be a millionaire, but she realized by analyzing her statement that the next 10 to 15 years were going to be critical earnings years.

Michele decided she wanted to earn as much as possible. This was not the time to scale back in her career or take a lower-paid job. That paycheck during her 50s was going to be important.

She set her sights on leveraging all her years of experience, learned the new dance of how to look for a job in the era of high technology, and landed a great job that even includes some travel. It's a well-deserved opportunity. She's young at heart, willing to tackle new challenges, and looking forward to a much larger Social Security retirement benefit at her full retirement age (FRA) than might have been the case if she hadn't taken a close look at her statement when she turned 50.

When was the last time you looked at your statement?

Michele's story is not intended to suggest that you go get a new job. It is to illustrate that each woman has her own unique journey. While we can appreciate someone else's story, we've each created our own. Social Security will only look at your situation when calculating your benefit. They are very clear about how they approach the math using your numbers.

By using the statement to your advantage, you can make better decisions. You might work longer or you might retire before finishing this book. Perhaps you were thinking about claiming your benefit at age 62, but looking at your statement shows you how much more you'll get by waiting until your FRA. If you are married or divorced, you can use your statement as your benchmark and see if you can get a larger monthly benefit as a spouse or ex-spouse.

For a few sheets of paper, your statement is the best tool you have in your retirement income toolbox. Sign in to www.SSA.gov/myaccount and open your statement. Read it thoroughly and use it to make good decisions for yourself and your future.

5

How You Get Your Social Security Retirement Benefit

As a social insurance program, we're required to pay into the system during our working years in order to get a benefit payment in our older, retirement years. You have to pay in today to receive benefits tomorrow, and you must qualify by meeting certain requirements. They aren't hard, and it doesn't require you to take a stress test or anything dramatic. Here is the general list of requirements individual workers must meet to become fully insured and qualify for and receive Social Security retirement benefits:

- You work for a covered employer who pays FICA taxes on your behalf

- You've earned 40 credits

- You've reached age 62

- You are a US citizen or qualifying Green Card holder

If you are a spouse or ex-spouse, you may qualify for benefits based on your spouse's record.

Working for a "covered" employer

Depending on the jobs you've held, you worked for a "covered" employer or an "uncovered" employer. "Covered" means that the employer paid into FICA – the Federal Insurance Contribution Act. "Uncovered" means your employer did not pay into FICA.

You have no say in how an employer is supporting the retirement of its workers. Today, 15 states have their own teacher's pension plans through a teacher's union. Rather than paying FICA taxes and participating in Social Security, the teachers and their union make contributions toward a pension plan. They work for an "uncovered" employer. There are other examples as well – if you work for certain other unions, for your state or local government, or any other job with an employer who supports a public pension.

An important note: Some companies and organizations are both covered employers, paying into Social Security, and sponsors of a pension plan. If your employer chooses to support both types of retirement plans, and as long as you are eligible for both, you will get a pension and your Social Security payment. That is a powerful combination for those who have that particular arrangement.

What exactly is FICA?

FICA, or the Federal Insurance Contributions Act, is the law that supports Social Security and Medicare funding. In order to pay future Social Security retirement claims, the Federal Government needed a way to collect taxes. Rather than hoping taxpayers would pay on their own accord, the Federal Government put the onus on employers: the employer must withhold a set percentage of every worker's salary and deposit it to Social Security. In addition, the employer must also make a payment out of their operating budget on behalf of every employee. It usually works out that the employee percentage is matched by the employer mandate – but not always.

Today, employees have 6.2% of their salary withheld and deposited to Social Security. Their covered employer matches that same percentage, directing an additional 6.2% into the coffers. During the great recession of 2008–2009, one lever the Federal Government pulled was to reduce the FICA tax payments, but only on the employee side. So, there was a two-year period where workers paid in 4.2%, but the employer still had to kick in the full 6.2%.

You need to earn 40 credits of work wages to qualify

The second requirement for qualifying for your own Social Security benefits is that you must earn 40 credits. You earn one credit for each quarter where you've earned over a minimum amount and paid FICA taxes on that income. Self-employment earnings count toward earning credits as does paid military duty.

In 2019, the minimum salary amount needed to earn one credit is $1,360. Whether you work full-time or part-time or have a seasonal job, as long as you earn at least this amount you will receive one credit.

You can earn up to a maximum of four credits per year, but to do so you need to earn at least $5,440 in 2019 (it was less in prior years and will be higher in future years). You do not need to work all 12 months, or a full year, to earn credits. When your employer reports your wages for the year, if they are higher than $5,440 you've earned all four credits. If you made, say, $3,000, you'll only earn two credits.

Do I need to work consecutive quarters or years?

One question that comes up frequently among women is whether they have to work 10 consecutive years in order to qualify for their benefits. The answer is: No.

You do not have to work consecutive quarters or consecutive years to earn your credits. When it comes to determining your Social Security eligibility, you need to amass 40 credits over your working career. Any eligible wages count toward earning credits throughout the years.

Age 62 opens the Social Security gate

I have yet to come across a woman in America who doesn't know the earliest age when they can get their Social Security retirement payment. "It's 62!" they shout out with glee. Yes, that is correct. Once we reach age 62, Social Security says we are close enough to retirement to get access to our retirement benefits. Many people, especially women, are anxiously awaiting their 62nd birthday so they can check out of their jobs and jump into the lap of luxury called retirement.

In 2017, roughly 51% of men and 56% of women claimed their benefit before their Full Retirement Age (33% of women claimed at the earliest age of 62). In 2013, 58% of men claimed before FRA and 64% of women did the same (40% of women claiming at 62).[8] While this is a welcome decrease in the numbers of early claims, too many still claim too early.

---

8   Social Security Administration (2018) *Annual Statistical Supplement, 2018: Table 6.B5: Number, average age, and percentage distribution, by sex and age, selected years 1940–2017.* https://SSA.gov/policy/docs/statcomps/supplement/2018/6b.html#table6.b5

The problem with claiming early is that it locks in a significant and permanent decrease in your monthly income – for the entire length of your retirement.

The question every woman should be asking is not, "How fast can I get my hot little hands on my Social Security check?" but rather, "Is there a catch to taking my Social Security at 62?" That is the critical question and the one that most don't know to ask.

When it looks too good to be true...

It's important to understand and remember that Social Security is designed to provide a modest amount of income in retirement. It's a safety net. Your personal retirement income payment is a calculated benefit called your Primary Insurance Amount or PIA.

The calculated value is the amount you will receive if you claim at your FRA. That's the age Social Security has determined to be your "official retirement age" whether you're retired from your job or not. Think of this age as the anchor for your benefit calculation.

Ideally, you want to claim your benefit when you reach your FRA. That's when you get your optimal amount of income. But what if you can't wait until 66 or 67? Say you lose your job or have to leave work to care for your spouse or aging parents? You gain access to Social Security once you've reached 62. The gate really does open. But you won't get the amount of money you thought you would. In fact, you will get a huge reduction in your monthly payments. And, it's a permanent reduction.

- If your FRA is 66, but you claim at 62, you'll get a 25% reduction in monthly income from Social Security

- If your FRA is 67, your penalty is a whopping 30% decrease in monthly income

It turns out claiming at 62 is a huge financial decision. And, sadly, I see many women who are so excited to quit their jobs and start collecting Social Security that they never bother to ask the question, "Is there a catch?"

When to retire and when to claim are two distinct decisions

It is quite common for women to think that when they retire they must immediately begin their Social Security payments. This is not the case. There are two distinct decisions that get made:

- When to quit your job

- When to begin Social Security payments

Keeping these two decisions separate helps to clarify the importance of Social Security as a key source of income for old age. If you want to retire at 60 or 62 – and so many women are absolutely burnt out from stressful jobs – that is one decision. How you will pay your bills takes a plan and some financial strategy. You might:

- Draw from some of your retirement savings accounts

- Have planned for early retirement and have a "retiring early" account at the ready

- Buy a fixed-income annuity that will pay out six or seven years of income

- Be married and your spouse's income can support your lifestyle

- Have paid off your mortgage and can use that new-found money to replace your wages

- Take on part-time work or a new job that is less stressful

Unfortunately, what happens all too often is that women leave their jobs and paychecks on a Friday and start their Social Security benefits on Monday. If they are younger than their FRA, they forever lock in lower (often much lower) monthly benefit amounts from Social Security. This is not an ideal strategy for most. They just didn't realize there were two different decisions to be made.

There's no "bumping up" with Social Security

Remember the telephone game we played when we were kids? The first person in a line would whisper a sentence to the next person. Then person number two whispered the sentence to person number three and so on to the end of the line. When you asked the last person what they were told, it rarely resembled the original sentence at all. Person number one might have said, "We're getting out of school at 2:00 today" but the last person might have heard, "They're closing school for two months." Not really the same thing at all.

That's what happens with the Social Security rules. One person thinks they understand the program; they tell the next, who thinks she's got it; she tells the next… and before you know it, Social Security is paying us each $2 million.

Many women have heard that they can claim reduced benefits when the gates open at 62 and their benefit amount will be bumped up to their full payment amount once they reach their FRA. That is incorrect. There is no bumping up in payments once you've claimed Social Security.

WHAT'S THE DEAL WITH... SOCIAL SECURITY FOR WOMEN?

Once you claim, you're locked in

The Social Security Administration is, in fact, clear in all of their documentation and examples and illustrations of how the system works. Once you're in, you're in. Whatever amount you're receiving is your permanent base payment. You will get slight increases each year for cost-of-living adjustments, or COLAs, but those are modest adjustments to help offset inflation, in the range of 1% to 3%.

There are two exceptions if you are willing to give up payments. You can stop your claim within the first 12 months and pay back all benefits. This is a "do-over." Alternately, at FRA you can suspend your benefits and restart them at age 70. This allows your reduced benefits to increase with delayed retirement credits. One additional situation may apply to some married women who have a smaller benefit and a larger spousal benefit. Your husband must be claiming before you can receive your spousal benefit. You might decide to claim your own reduced benefit as early as age 62, then get your spousal top-up later, after your husband claims his benefit. (See Section 2A on claiming for those who are married.)

Think carefully and strategically about whether claiming at 62 is the best path for you to take. You are, in fact, making a monumental financial decision in your early 60s that will impact your income well into your 80s and 90s, and you may be among the growing population of women who will celebrate reaching age 100.

Social Security retirement benefits for citizens and Green Card holders

The final general rule for securing your retirement benefits is that you must be an American citizen. This is often obvious, but with such interesting diversity among women, this question does come up more and more frequently. I mainly hear it from naturalized citizens who have brought their foreign-born parents to live with them, or from foreign-born workers who are married to American-born spouses, or from permanent non-residents.

In order to be eligible for Social Security, you personally – and each individual collecting – must be an American citizen or a permanent legal resident. For those internationals who have become permanent residents of the US and hold a Green Card, if you otherwise meet the rules of eligibility, you are entitled to Social Security benefits. You can get them as an individual worker who earned at least 40 credits or as a spouse of an eligible worker.

To make certain you know the rules specific to your situation, anyone holding a Green Card should talk with Social Security or with an immigration lawyer. If you have earned Social Security benefits, you'll want to make sure you and your spouse are collecting them. In most cases, if you are a permanent resident of the US, all of the same Social Security rules for benefits that apply for citizens also apply to you.

6

Two Important News Flashes: Math Is Involved And It's Not Really Your Money

As a social insurance program, your insurance benefit requires the same expertise that other types of insurance programs do: great math minds and actuaries. This is not a bad thing. It's just that most of us have no idea what actuaries do and how they come up with their estimates. There are several interesting situations a Social Security actuary has to balance when forecasting the sustainability of the program and making sure that you get your monthly payment:

- How can all beneficiaries rely on a guaranteed income?

- What happens when a person's situation changes (from single to married, married to widowed, etc.)?

- When exactly should someone be considered retired?

- What adjustments should be considered for wage inflation?

- How much of a reduction should be made for those who want to claim early?

In other words, actuaries are concerned with how to make an insurance program sustainable and fair for decades into the future.

Finding your Full Retirement Age

The actuaries at Social Security estimate the total benefit amount each recipient could receive if they live for a long time in retirement. They anchor these estimates at Full Retirement Age (FRA). If you decide to claim your benefit early, you can, but since your payments would have to stretch out over a longer period of time you'll get a reduced monthly amount.

It used to be that age 65 was the magic date for everyone. Today, each person's FRA is based on the year they were born. Here is a partial list:

Year you were born	Full Retirement Age (FRA)
1943–1954	66
1955	66 and 2 months
1956	66 and 4 months
1957	66 and 6 months
1958	66 and 8 months
1959	66 and 10 months
1960 and later	67

Find the year you were born and see when Social Security deems you to be retired. If you were born in 1958, you reach FRA the month and year when you'll be exactly 66 years and 8 months. If your birthday is June 3, 1958, you reach your FRA in February 2025. You do not reach FRA in June 2024, when you turn 66. There is no rounding off FRA ages. In this example, you do not qualify for full retirement benefits until you are 8 months past your 66th birthday.

What if your birthday is on the first of the month? In that case, your FRA is anchored in the previous month. And if your birthday is January 1st of any given year, your FRA was reached in December of the previous year. Yes, really.

Your decisions matter

When you decide to claim your benefit can have a significant impact on your financial stability throughout retirement. If you claim your benefit before reaching your FRA, your monthly payment will be permanently reduced – by as much as 25% or 30%. Ouch. That is a dramatic drop in benefit amounts. So, you have to ask yourself, "Can I really afford to give up ⅓ of my monthly Social Security paycheck?" Most of us would answer, "No!" to that question.

If you can wait to claim your Social Security benefit until after reaching your FRA, you get a "bonus" amount. Your benefit will increase 8% per year that you delay receipt until you reach age 70. This bonus money is called "delayed retirement credits", and you are eligible to receive them any month after FRA until age 70.

Wage adjustments make a difference

Your income from the 1970s does not have the same buying power as the wages you are earning today. So, how can decades of back wages be adjusted to better reflect current prices?

To calculate your personal benefit, Social Security will look at your entire wage history. Each year's wage amount will then be adjusted by a specific factor that is "actuarially equivalent" to the strength of the dollar in the year you turn(ed) 60. Any wages earned from age 60 onward are used as is. Your highest 35 years of these indexed wages will be used in your personal benefit calculation. The highest 35 years of wages are tallied up to a grand total, then divided by 35 years and again by 12 months per year to give you your Average Indexed Monthly Earnings (AIME) number.

An example of calculating AIME

Let's say that, after adjusting 45 years of work history for wage inflation, you pull out the highest 35 years, and total them up. Using an example, the total value is $2,950,800. Many women will see their total inflation-adjusted earnings top $1 million.

Here's how to calculate AIME:

($2,950,800 total indexed wages) / (35 years) = $84,309 average annual wages / (12 months per year) = $7,026 per month

AIME is the first calculation in determining your insurance benefit. It is not your social insurance payment amount.

Calculating a Primary Insurance Amount

Your AIME now needs to be split into three tiers to calculate your Primary Insurance Amount (PIA). These tiers, or bands, are determined by the actuaries and are adjusted every year. If you reach age 62 in 2019, these are your tiers:

- 90% of the first $926 of your AIME

- 32% of AIME that falls between $926 and $5,583

- 15% of any remaining AIME over $5,583

Returning to the example above for the person who has an AIME of $7,026, her PIA calculates to roughly $2,539. If her AIME was $3,500 instead of $7,026, her calculated PIA would be about $1,656.

	2019 Parameters	AIME = $7,026	AIME = $3,500
1st tier	90% of $926	$833	$833
2nd tier	32% of AIME between $5,583 and $926	$1,490	$823
3rd tier	15% of AIME above $5,583	$216	n/a
Primary Insurance Amount		**$2,539**	**$1,656**

This is the general idea behind calculating Social Security's insurance benefit. The calculations are squarely focused on fairness based on your own eligibility (you earned 40 credits or more) and your unique work and wage history. The rest is just some math.

When your money is not really your money

You pay real dollars into Social Security when working for a covered employer so that in retirement you'll receive a calculated benefit. The cash you pay in goes directly out to pay for current retirees' benefits.

It is important to remember a key concept behind Social Security: it was not set up as a welfare program. It was and is a self-funding, pay-in-now-to-get-benefits-later program. You're earning credits for participation, and in return you'll get benefits in retirement.

Paying your fair share

The dollars that come out of every paycheck are not specifically earmarked for you. The fact that you are paying in your share counts as credits, or "chits in the bank," for your future benefits.

Sometimes people are quite frustrated by that fact. "I paid in tens of thousands of dollars over my career! Why can't I get all of that back? It is my money!" No, it's not. And it never was.

Here's how to look at your share of paying into Social Security. For anyone who lives a long time in retirement, they get a return of their contributions and then some. In fact, those who live 30 years in retirement can receive as much as two-and-a-half times more than the contributions made by themselves and their employers.

A simple example illustrates the power of the program

Keeping in mind that my example is not an exact calculation and is meant only to illustrate the power of the Social Security program, here are some rough numbers to show you the advantage of Social Security retirement benefits:

- Assume you worked for 40 years for a covered employer and met the taxable wage base every year. Your first job was in 1980 and your last paycheck was at the end of 2019.

- You would have paid into Social Security around $185,000, not adjusted for inflation.

- Your employer would have paid in roughly the same amount, or slightly higher. That's another $185,000.

- Contributions into Social Security would be about $370,000 made on your behalf.

- Now, let's adjust for inflation using Social Security's index inflation factors for 1980–2019. In 2019 dollars, you've paid just under $300,000 into Social Security and your employer has matched that amount, for a total of $600,000 in inflation-adjusted dollars.

Any way you look at these numbers, they are very large. This is a significant amount of money being put into the program from you and your employer and, in turn, paid out to current recipients of Social Security, including your parents, grandparents, and many other loved ones.

Living many years in retirement

Let's now say that you live for 30 years in retirement, from 67 to 97. This is not out of the realm of possibility for many women. Every month during your 30-year retirement, you will get a Social Security payment – no questions asked.

- Assuming you earned the taxable wage base every year, your highest 35 years of earnings will be used to calculate your Social Security benefit. Your PIA is about $2,800.

- After 30 years, you'll have received just shy of $1.5 million! (That's using a straight-line annual inflation factor of 2.5%.)

- This means that you and your employer paid in roughly $600,000, yet you get $1.5 million in benefits. That's more than 2½ times the amount that was contributed on your behalf.

- What if you only live for 25 years in retirement? Your benefits reach approximately $1.2 million, or twice the amount that was contributed on your behalf.

This is the power behind the social insurance program. And this one in particular is remarkable in that it insures you if you live a long life. You'll "recoup" your contributions if you live eight years into retirement, and the full amount that was contributed on your behalf comes back to you after about 15 years.

Anyone who has reached about age 80 has been repaid, if you want to look at it like that. And, those who are in their late 80s and 90s and 100s... well, that is one heck of a good deal on their insurance policy!

The only problem here is that you have no way of knowing if you'll live to a ripe old age. That's why it's called insurance.

The success of Social Security

You will receive a payment each and every month that you live in retirement. Your spouse will also receive a nice tidy check throughout their retirement. And from the 80- and 90-year-old's perspective, it's a darn good thing to be getting these insurance payments.

Among elderly Social Security beneficiaries:

- 48% of married couples receive 50% or more of their income from Social Security

- 69% of unmarried persons receive 50% or more of their income from Social Security[9]

One of the core tenets of the Social Security Act of 1935 was to keep America's elderly out of poverty. The program was not designed to provide former workers and their spouses with great riches. It was meant to keep food on the table in old age. In that regard, Social Security has been, and continues to be, a wildly successful program. And, frankly, there are very few Americans who could survive in retirement without this critical social insurance program in place. Would you?

---

9   Social Security Fact Sheet for December 2018.

7
How Much Do You Really Need To Know?

It is important that all women understand key elements of the Social Security program. No, you don't have to be a math genius. In fact, if you simply download your statement and look at your numbers, that will be sufficient for most planning purposes. The math has already been done based on your real wage history.

What you do need to know are some of the facts about the program and how your own personal work history can make a difference in your retirement income. The more you understand the more confident you'll be that you're making the best decisions you can before you claim your benefit.

WHAT'S THE DEAL WITH... SOCIAL SECURITY FOR WOMEN?

One lady I met walked around with a retirement countdown clock on her smartphone! She had a tough, demanding, stressful job, and she could hardly wait to retire. She knew she wanted to claim at her Full Retirement Age, but it would be hard. She found a "countdown to retirement" app and it was motivating. She still had more than 700 days until retirement, but it made her happy to watch the daily countdown: 732 days, 8 hours, 41 minutes, 06 seconds. Yes, it really was this exact.

Ten important factors to consider before claiming your benefit

1. **Your monthly check will be cut severely if you claim at 62:** Up to a whopping 30%. Is it worth it to claim early if you are going to lock in permanently reduced income? It may be that you have no choice, or that you have plenty of other money. It's about understanding the implications and consequences of drawing so early. You don't want to regret the decision when you're 85.

2. **Your own work history drives your benefit amount.** If you were fortunate enough to earn a lot of money in your career, that's great. The maximum payout is just over $2,800 per month if you reached FRA in 2019. If you had a career that paid less, you will receive a benefit based on your earnings.

3. **You need 40 credits to qualify.** Don't stop working if you have 36 credits and want to claim on your own work record. You need 40 credits to get your own benefits. (Generally, that means working during 10 years when you paid FICA taxes on a certain amount of income.)

4. **The maximum number of credits is four per year.** In 2019, the minimum amount you must earn from covered employment is $5,440 to earn four credits.

5. **Don't worry if you have moved in and out of the workforce.** Many women come in and out of the paid workforce during a 40-to-50-year career. Whether you stepped out of work when you had babies, stayed home during their teenage years, or cared for an aging parent or a sick spouse, partner, or friend, there are any number of reasons why you may have gaps in your work history. Social Security will include only your highest 35 years. They do not have to be consecutive years.

6. **Social Security will look at you in one of four categories.** You are an individual worker, a spouse, an ex-spouse, or a surviving spouse. You will be in one of these categories at the point when you claim your benefits. You may move in and out of all four categories during your life.

7. **You only get one benefit at a time.** It will be the highest benefit available to you at the time of your claim. If you fall into the categories of individual

worker and spouse, you'll get one benefit check and it's from the category that gives you the most money per month.

8. **If you are in a same-sex marriage, the same benefits and rules apply.** Married is married from Social Security's perspective. If you have a legal marriage or a qualifying common-law marriage, you are eligible to claim your spousal benefits, your ex-spouse benefits, or your surviving spouse benefits. You'll receive one benefit at a time, and it's the highest one for which you are eligible.

9. **If you can wait to claim until after your FRA, you'll increase your monthly payment.** Those who wait can increase their monthly income by as much as 24% or 32%. But you need a good strategy in place to take advantage of this, and it often includes working until 70 and/or having a lot of money saved for the purpose of retiring well before claiming Social Security.

10. **Staking your claim is all but irrevocable.** There are only a couple of ways to undo your claim. You'll have to pay back all of the money you've received from Social Security or stop payments for several years, and this is not an option for most women. Be extra mindful about making your claim. Make sure you really want to start those benefits checks when you push the button.

Start with SSA.gov to look for your situation and options

It can take a while to figure out how your specific benefit is going to work. This is especially true if you've been married a couple of times. Before you think about claiming, do some additional reading about your situation, and spend some time on www.SSA.gov. The information is sweeping in nature and tries to address every kind of situation a woman in America could find herself in.

If you are a woman with any sort of special circumstances, there is likely information on www.SSA.gov to address your situation, including:

- If you want to remarry after your spouse dies, what are the implications for your surviving spouse benefits?

- If your spouse is or was incarcerated, what does that do to your benefits?

- What if you are a disabled military veteran? There is a section that addresses that situation.

- If your husband is significantly older than you and the two of you have children, are there benefits for the children?

- Have you been a victim of domestic violence? There are special rules that can help you apply for a new Social Security Number.

Use www.SSA.gov as your go-to resource. Sometimes life can get pretty messy. Use this website to find information, phone numbers, or branch offices where you can discuss your situation with an agent.

PART TWO

THE SOCIAL SECURITY CLAIMING CATEGORIES

Social security has four claiming categories: You are a spouse (Section A), an ex-spouse (Section B), a surviving spouse (Section C), or an individual (Section D).

Find the section that applies to you and read about the rules and examples of women who are in the same category.

If you will be receiving a public pension, your Social Security payments may be reduced. See Section E for information about the Windfall Elimination Provision (WEP), which can reduce your own benefits, and the Government Pension Offset (GPO), which can reduce your spousal benefits.

SECTION A

Overview for married women: the basics for happily married couples

8

Married Couples – Coordinating Benefits And Claiming Decisions Are A Must

Ah, marriage. Isn't it grand? I ask audiences all around the country to raise their hands if they are part of a happily married couple. There are roars of laughter. A few hands go up right away, and a lot of wives elbow their husbands and loudly whisper, "Raise your hand! We are happily married!" It livens up the crowd and keeps them engaged in what could otherwise be a daunting topic: Social Security benefits for married couples.

This section of the book includes a several examples of how spouses at different ages and in different situations need to think about their claiming strategies and the timing of their claims. You can find more examples and a checklist and action plan for married women on my *Boomer Retirement Briefs* blog at https://boomerretirementbriefs.com.

First, let's look at the general rules for married couples. This should give you a good foundation of how Social Security works for married couples before diving into specific scenarios.

Recognizing homemakers and mothers

One of the most remarkable features of the Social Security retirement program is that from the beginning, the architects of the law recognized the role of the married woman. Thinking back to the 1930s, that was quite a progressive idea. Social Security clearly acknowledged a wife's role in the household and that she deserved her own paycheck in retirement. That women only get half of their husbands' benefit amounts... well, that could have been more generous!

The rationale for at-home moms and homemakers to receive a paycheck at all stems from the acknowledgment that it was the couple – the happily married couple – who together made a successful economic unit. If Mom wasn't home taking care of the brood of children, then Dad wouldn't be able to work and produce and support the company. It was the power of the duo that contributed to the economic engine of the country, each in his and her own way. At the point of retirement, Congress recognized that both had been working all along. One outside the home, one inside the home.

The basic rules for spouses

The starting point for figuring out benefits for married couples assumes the husband was the wage earner, the wife the homemaker. When the husband reached 65, he retired and started collecting Social Security. At that time his non-wage-earning wife would become eligible for a retirement benefit once she reached age 65. (It wasn't until 1956 that women and wives could claim early at age 62.) She would receive 50% of his Primary Insurance Amount (PIA) when she turned 65, or she would get a reduced payment if she claimed early.

If a husband was entitled to $500 per month at his Full Retirement Age (FRA) of 65, his wife was entitled to $250 per month once she reached 65. The total household income would be $750. It was relatively simple and easy to implement spousal benefits back in the 1930s and 1940s.

A turning point for wives: World War II

In 1941, we entered the Second World War. Women were asked to both run their homes and take on jobs for the war effort. It turns out that this one request, for more women to join the ranks of the working, set the stage for increased Social Security complexity – an unintended consequence. When women started working outside the home, they found that they were capable, valued on the job, and empowered to have some input into the financial success of the household. By the time they reached retirement age of 65, it was the 1970s and 1980s. These working women qualified for their own retirement benefits as well as their spousal benefits, and things got interesting:

In the more traditional situation, one group of women worked temporarily, on an as-needed basis. Some worked to support the war effort. Others worked for a few years before they got married, or perhaps from time to time to help with household bills or extras. Over their working years, they did not earn 40 credits. They were not eligible for Social Security benefits on their own record, but they did indeed qualify as spouses. This group of women would receive half of their husbands' PIAs when they turned 65. If he got $800, she got $400.

There was also an emerging group of women who worked outside the home for long enough to earn their 40 credits. So, on their own, they independently qualified for retirement benefits *and* spousal benefits. Would they receive their own benefit or their spousal benefit or both? There is no "double-dipping" when it comes to Social Security, so they weren't going to get both benefits. The rules state when you are eligible for two benefits at the same time, you receive only one of them – the higher one. And, in in the case of wives, it may be made up of two parts:

- Assume your PIA is $500 per month, but your spousal benefit is $800 each month. Your higher calculated value is $800. Technically, you receive your own $500 from your work record, plus a spousal "top-up" of $300. The combination of payments gets you to your highest calculated benefit.

- Now assume you are eligible for a monthly benefit of $950 on your own work record, and your spousal benefit is $800 per month. Now what? Well, again, you'll get the one, single highest calculated benefit for which you are eligible. In this case, hubby still out-earned you. (His PIA is $1,600 per month.) But your own work record was high enough that you are entitled to more than half of his. Therefore, you'll receive $950 per month, the result of your own work record.

- In more recent years, we know that some wives have out-paced their husbands' earnings histories. Let's assume one of these women's monthly benefit at her FRA is $2,400. Her husband, who also had a good career, has a calculated benefit of $2,000 per month. Half of his is $1,000, so she will not receive the lower spousal benefit. Her benefit will be her $2,400 per month. Her husband's benefit will be his $2,000 per month. In this case, each spouse's highest benefit is based on their own work history. Neither is eligible for spousal benefits.

Today, Social Security doesn't care who the higher earner is or if you get more on your spousal benefit or your own record. The important considerations for a couple are:

- There is a higher earner and a lower earner

- Both members of the couple are entitled to a retirement paycheck

- Each member of the couple is entitled to one benefit at a time and it's the highest for which they are eligible at the time

Same-sex married couples are married in the eyes of Social Security

The Social Security spousal rules are "spouse agnostic". This is an important factor for same-sex married couples. When the section of the Defense of Marriage Act that excluded same-sex couples from marrying was finally repealed in June 2015, same-sex spouses were immediately covered under Social Security's existing provisions. It was one small victory for those who otherwise had to fight long and hard for the benefits of marriage equality.

In general, to be eligible for spousal benefits, all couples must be married to their current spouse for 12 months. However, for same-sex couples who had been in civil or domestic partnerships because they could not legally marry, they may not have to wait for the 12 months to start receiving spousal payments. Their pre-marriage arrangement may be recognized as qualifying time so that benefits can start immediately. The SSA strongly encourages older same-sex couples who are now married to file for benefits right away so they can assess whether they are due back benefit payments. That includes any spousal benefits as well as any payments that would have been made to children or other eligible family members.

If you have questions about the benefits you can receive as a same-sex couple, read the information on www.SSA.gov. You may prefer to make an appointment at your local Social Security office or call for a consultation. There's not a lot of information on www.SSA.gov for same-sex married couples, but it's a good place to start your research.

When you are eligible to claim benefits, if your situation is relatively simple, you can apply for your own benefits or for spousal benefits using the online application at www.SSA.gov.

Spousal benefits are hitched to the wage earner

If you have your own work record you can file for your benefits when it works best in your retirement income plan. However, you can only file for spousal benefits when your spouse is already claiming their benefit. You and your spouse come as a packaged set. Similar to filing your taxes jointly, your spousal benefits work like riding a tandem bike. You both need to be on the bike and pedaling to move forward.

If your only benefit is the spousal benefit, you cannot claim spousal payments until your higher-earning spouse is claiming their benefit *and* you have reached at least age 62. No one gets their Social Security retirement benefits before the age of 62. (Surviving spouse benefits are a different story, discussed in later chapters.)

Let's say your husband is three years older than you. If he waits until his FRA of 67 before he claims his benefits, you'll have to wait until you are 64. If, on the other hand, he wants to claim at his earliest age of 62, you are not yet eligible for your spousal benefit; you are only 59 at this point. You have to wait until you reach 62, three years later, to file for your spousal benefits.

Furthermore, you can wait until after your spouse claims their benefit before you claim. Why? It might be a good idea to wait until your FRA before you claim to get the maximum payment that you are eligible to receive.

Spousal benefit examples

Let's look at several examples for Sally Snowflake and Richard Raine. They have been married for more than

12 months. He was born in 1960, she in 1963. They each reach their FRA at 67.

Sally does not qualify for her own worker's benefit, but she will receive a spousal benefit. The maximum spousal benefit Sally is eligible for is 50% of Richard's PIA. She'll only get the maximum if she waits until her FRA.

Here are several possible scenarios Sally and Richard can consider (all numbers are approximate):

Richard's Claiming Age	His Benefit Amount	Sally's Claiming Age	Her Benefit Amount	Comments
67	$2,000	67	$1,000	Each wait until FRA to claim; she has to wait 3 years after he claims
62	$1,400	67	$1,000	Even though he claimed early, her benefit is based on his PIA at her FRA
67	$2,000	64	$750	They claim at the same time; she's younger than FRA
65	$1,733	62	$650	Both want to retire early and claim early; both amounts are permanently reduced
70	$2,480	67	$1,000	He claims at 70, so she must wait until he claims to claim her spousal benefit

What you see in these examples is how married couples have to think about the timing of their claim in a coordinated fashion. If he waits to claim until his FRA, she cannot get any Social Security retirement benefits until she's at least age 64. Maybe that's best for their plan. Maybe they decide they want to get as much income as possible, so they will both wait until their FRAs or even until he reaches age 70 to claim.

Two big points here for the spouses:

1. Spouses only get half of their spouses' PIAs. It does not matter when the wage earner collects – before FRA, at FRA, or after FRA. The spouse's benefit calculation is still based on the higher wage earner's PIA.

2. Whenever either person in the couple claims early, they get a reduction in their benefit amount. And it can be a steep reduction if either claim at age 62.

Topping up later

What if you have a benefit coming to you on your own work record and you are eligible for a spousal "top-up"? In this case, you can choose to claim at any time from age 62 onward on your own work record. If your spouse is not already claiming, you can only stake your claim on your work record. The timing for receiving the topped-up portion of your spousal benefit depends on your spouse. Eventually, when your spouse claims, you are then eligible to get your top-up for the spousal benefit.

An example might help here:

- You have reached your FRA of 67 and decide to claim your retirement benefit. Your husband is also at his FRA of 67 but wants to wait until 70 to claim, as he is the higher earner. Your full retirement benefit is $800 per month; his is $2,400 per month.

- When you claim at your FRA, you will receive your own full retirement benefit of $800 per month. Your calculated spousal benefit is half of his, or $1,200 per month. Your spousal top-up will be $400 per month. You cannot access the top-up yet since your husband is not also claiming. Remember the tandem bike. In this situation, you start out riding your own bike.

- Three years later, your husband is ready to claim. He gets out the tandem bike and you both ride together. Your spousal top-up now becomes available. Your $800 per month continues to be paid, and you request your extra $400 per month in top-up benefits. Your monthly payments increase to $1,200 per month.

- Meanwhile, your husband's $2,400 per month has increased by 8% per year since he waited until 70 to claim. His benefit gets the boost of a 24% higher monthly income, or approximately $2,976. (Your top-up is calculated on his original PIA, not his bonus payment amount.)

Sure, it's a little complicated here for spouses. Just remember you can't get a fully-loaded, topped-up spousal benefit unless and until both of you are claiming.

Claiming early will cost you

One last key consideration of the rules for spouses has to do with when you claim your benefit. Your FRA is based on the year you were born. Your PIA, or anchor, is calculated based on that year.

If you claim at any month before reaching FRA, you will lock in a permanent reduction in your benefit. Permanent reductions apply whether you are the higher-earning spouse who claims benefits early or if you are the spouse who claims spousal benefits early.

When you claim early on your own work record, the reduction formula is split into two parts: a reduction factor for the months between age 62 and age 65 (the original FRA for everyone) and a different reduction factor for the months after 65 until your FRA. The reduction calculation is:

- 5/9 of 1% for each month during the first 36 months (20% reduction)

- 5/12 of 1% for each month that falls in the next 24 months (10% further reduction)

Reductions for spouses' early benefits versus for workers

Here's what happens to your spousal benefit if you claim it before your FRA. For each month you claim early, your payment is reduced by a specific percentage that is higher than it would be on a worker's record:

- 25/36 of 1% for each month during the first 36 months (25% reduction)

- 5/12 of 1% for each month that falls in the next 24 months (10% further reduction)

If a spouse with an FRA of 67 claims at 62, she'll get a full 35% reduction of her spousal benefit. Her starting point is half of his PIA. So, if his PIA is $2,000 per month, her spousal benefit at FRA is $1,000 per month. But, if she claims at 62, she'll only receive $650 per month – a whopping 35% reduction.

That's not to say she shouldn't claim at 62 if that's what works for the couple. There are lots of reasons why a wife might want to claim early:

- She may be significantly younger than her spouse and they may want to spend their early retirement years traveling together

- She may need to or want to care for her grandchildren

- She may need to provide care for a sick parent, spouse or partner

- They have saved for the purpose of retiring early, and getting some Social Security income helps the couple fulfill their dream

The bottom line is to make an early claiming decision with your eyes wide open. Understand the permanence of the decision and that you generally can't undo the decision. It is a lot of income to give up every month during a 30-year retirement. Make sure you know what your choices are and the consequences of the decisions you make. Way too often women say that they didn't know. Well, now you know.

A note about the Restricted Application

Married women who were born in the early 1950s seem to know that they have access to more benefits than just their own. If you were born before January 2, 1954 and are married and filing taxes jointly, there was a loophole in the Social Security laws. It allowed one spouse to claim just her spousal benefit at her FRA.

Her own work record was allowed to grow 8% per year with delayed retirement credits.

This meant that some married women could claim half of their spouses' PIAs when they reached age 66, then wait until 70 to request their own payments. This gave them four years of extra Social Security payments *plus* a much higher benefit when they reached age 70.

This strategy was called "claim some now, claim more later". And that is clearly not what Social Security's goals are. Therefore, this unintended consequence was shut down as part of the Bipartisan Budget Act of 2015. I mention it here only because there are still women who could get extra benefits if they were born at the right time and if their spouse is already claiming.

Note: The Restricted Application also works for husbands if they meet the age requirement. A husband can claim just his spousal benefit if his spouse is claiming and he wants to delay his own claim until age 70.

Every wife's situation is different

There are no hard and fast rules for when the best time is to claim your own Social Security. In the chapters that follow in this section, you'll meet several married women, all with different backgrounds, situations, and earnings histories. See if your situation is similar to those of any of these women. Read their stories and see what options they might have when thinking about how and when to claim their Social Security benefits.

You'll find more cases and an action plan and checklist on *Boomer Retirement Briefs* at https://boomerretirementbriefs.com.

While there can be many routes to take, making the final decisions are based on two key elements: a full retirement income plan and a pretty good idea of what to do with your time in retirement.

In the following chapters you'll meet these interesting couples who have key decisions to make:

- Sandy and Steve assumed traditional divisions of labor in the household. What will Sandy's choices be for her Social Security?

- Mike and Melissa are an unusual couple in the Baby Boomer generation. She's the doctor, and he'd be a starving artist without her.

- Dwight and Amanda met when he started working in the same company where she had been employed for years. She's already claiming Social Security. Will she be eligible for a spousal top-up?

9

The "Traditional" Husband And Wife Arrangement: He's Older And The Earner

Sandy and Steve are what one might call a traditional married couple with traditional divisions of labor in the household. They got married in their mid-20s and started a family right away. Over the next 12 years, they had four children. Steve's first job was in sales. He traveled a lot and they relocated several times as he was offered promotions and moved up the corporate ladder. It was an easy decision for them that Sandy would be in charge of the home and kids while Steve pursued career advancement. Sandy always wanted to stay home with her kids, be involved with their schools, and use her creative and artistic skills.

As the kids got older and more independent, Sandy had time to do more volunteer work in her community. She started a reading program at the library and helped a friend start a cycling team that raises money for children's cancer research. She loved to host social events at her house, from book clubs and ladies' painting parties to backyard barbeques and big family holiday celebrations.

Both she and Steve knew that her role was important and that they were better off as a family with this arrangement.

Will their plan for retirement work?

Because Steve's promotions came fairly frequently, they could make saving for retirement a focus. Steve took advantage of his 401(k) at work and Sandy set up and funded her own IRAs (individual retirement accounts) over the years.

Their plan is for Steve to work until at least age 65, when he'll be eligible for Medicare. There is a three-year age difference between them, so they'll have to figure out options for Sandy's health insurance if he retires before she is eligible for Medicare at 65. The question they have is: should Steve plan to work until 68 instead of retiring at 65? Will that be the best plan for them when thinking about their Social Security benefits and making sure they have health care coverage?

An initial look at Social Security

There are a number of factors to take into consideration for each person, not the least of which is how much of a spousal benefit Sandy is entitled to. Since Sandy worked for only four years before staying home to raise her family, she does not qualify for Social Security retirement benefits on her own work record; however, she is entitled as a spouse to claim on Steve's work record. When she reaches her own Full Retirement Age (FRA) of 66 and 10 months, she can begin receiving 50% of Steve's Primary Insurance Amount (PIA). He'll have to be claiming his benefit already, but as he's three years older, that may work out well.

Another factor is that Steve's retirement date can be different from when he claims his Social Security benefit. He could retire at, say, 63. As long as they have other means to pay their living expenses, he would not have to claim Social Security until a future date. Just because one retires from a job, or is asked to retire, this does not mean they have to tap Social Security at the same time.

It's not just about the numbers

A closer look at Sandy and Steve's numbers will set the foundation for decision-making. Steve reaches FRA at 66 years, 4 months. Sandy reaches her FRA when she gets to 66 and 10 months. Here's a look at some of their combined claiming options (all numbers are approximate):

Steve's age when claiming	Monthly benefit	Sandy's age when claiming	Monthly benefit	Total Social Security income
At his FRA: 66 and 4 months	$2,200	At age 63	$780	$2,980
At age 65	$2,000	At age 62	$725	$2,725
At age 68	$2,490	At age 65	$930	$3,420
At age 70	$2,845	At age 67	$1,100	$3,945

As with most married couples, there's not a clear best answer regarding when to claim benefits. There are a number of important factors Sandy and Steve should think about before making their decision, including:

- When does Steve want to retire? What is realistic with his job, and is the company going to keep him on the job until he reaches 68?

- What other resources do they have to tap into if they are going to wait to claim Social Security benefits until Steve's FRA or later?

- What options will they have for Sandy's health insurance before she turns 65 and is eligible to join Medicare? How much will that cost, and do they have the money?

- Even though waiting until 70 gives Steve the highest monthly benefit, it does not change Sandy's monthly benefit. The maximum amount Sandy can receive is 50% of Steve's PIA, or $1,100 per month.

- If Steve starts to claim at 65, Sandy will be 62 and eligible to claim as well. However, she'll receive the lowest amount of her spousal benefit – approximately $725 per month.

- Steve can still claim a reduced benefit at 65 and Sandy could wait until she turns 65, increasing her monthly benefit to $930 per month.

- The decision Steve makes will also affect Sandy if she becomes a widow. As a widow, Sandy would lose her spousal benefit but would receive the amount Steve was collecting. Thinking about the survivor's benefit is a key consideration for all couples. (More about survivor benefits in later chapters.)

Making the decision is not so easy

This situation illustrates a number of financial realities for women who have been in the traditional household role. One is that the most Social Security income at-home wives can receive is half of their husbands' PIAs. That certainly helps any financial budget, but keep in mind there can be several years before the wife begins collecting benefits.

Also bear in mind that it can be challenging to make the best decision when the benefit amounts are so different. On the surface, it looks obvious that Steve should wait until age 70 to claim, even though that means

Sandy cannot get any income from Social Security until she turns 67. In that scenario, though, she cannot claim spousal benefits until Steve has made his claim.

Their original question was whether Steve could retire at 65 and start both Social Security and Medicare. If he takes this action, and Sandy claims at the same time (she'll be 62), they would receive $1,220 less in monthly income than if they wait until he is 70 and she 67. Sandy could still wait to claim her spousal benefit until she was 65, but that only increases her benefit by about $200 per month.

A complete retirement income plan is essential

The decision cannot be made by just looking at a table of Social Security combinations. This couple needs a comprehensive retirement income plan. They'll have to weigh their Social Security decisions in context of all their other resources:

• It might be that they have millions saved for retirement, so they'll wait until they reach 70 and 67 to maximize their Social Security benefit

• Perhaps Steve decides to work until 70 to delay claiming

- With putting four children through college, maybe they haven't saved as much as they will need for retirement and will need Social Security to start right away

Based on Steve's question, and his clear desire to retire earlier, it may be a better decision for him to claim at 65 or at his FRA. This allows them to draw less from their own assets, hopefully preserving some as a family legacy.

Realistically, even if Steve decided it would be best to continue working, his company may have other ideas and his employment could end sooner than planned. The key is to look at different options based on their overall retirement income plan.

Summary

Is it better for Sandy and Steve to prioritize time or maximize their Social Security income? Each couple has to decide how to balance their opportunities. There is no bad decision so long as each person understands the trade-offs.

Married women who do not qualify for Social Security retirement benefits on their own work records should keep a few key points in mind:

- You are entitled to your own retirement benefits on your spouse's work record.

- You get 50% of their PIA if you claim at your FRA. You'll get less if you claim earlier, and you will not get a higher amount if you wait until after your FRA.

- You cannot claim your spousal benefit until your spouse has claimed their own benefit. The two of you must come as a dancing duo into Social Security retirement benefits.

10
She's The Doctor; He's The Starving Artist

Mike and Melissa are a somewhat unusual couple among the older group of Baby Boomers. They got married young, back in the 1970s, and she's been the sole breadwinner for 40 years. She's a physician and the department chair at a large hospital system. He was an at-home dad and has been "dabbling" at art for decades. They are funny, smart, and still in love after 45 years together. They are both tradition-busters and have been ahead of their time through their years together. Melissa was born in December 1952. She's still working and plans to continue to work for at least a few more years, likely until age 70. She signed up for Medicare in 2017 as she was turning 65. Mike was born in 1954, so he's a couple of years younger.

Mike posed the original question that got our discussion going: "My wife is the higher earner and I don't qualify for Social Security. Is it possible for a 'trophy husband' to get anything from Social Security? If so, can I start now?"

Non-wage-earning spouses, even husbands, get benefits

Well, yes and no. In short, Mike will indeed get his own retirement benefit as a "trophy husband", but he cannot claim his spousal benefit until Melissa claims her benefit. He will be eligible for half of Melissa's Primary Insurance Amount (PIA) once he reaches his Full Retirement Age (FRA) at 66.

They were very surprised to learn that Mike could get any amount of Social Security at all, as he didn't work long enough to accumulate 40 credits. Melissa said that she knew that she had to sign up for Medicare as soon as she was approaching age 65, but she had never heard that non-wage-earning spouses – and husbands, no less – would be eligible for spousal benefits.

She is in good company. The vast majority of non-wage-earning spouses have no idea they are entitled to their own Social Security retirement benefits.

Mike was very happy to learn that he is entitled to up to half of Melissa's benefit amount. He felt somewhat valued and validated that his role in being the "trophy husband and all-around great dad" (his description, not hers, but she did agree after a short pause) was recognized at retirement. And, they are both delighted that their household income will be higher than they thought once they are both claiming Social Security. In fact, they will see about 33% more income from Social Security while both are alive. That was quite a bonus to learn about, and now they are rethinking when Melissa might retire.

When should she claim?

Melissa reached her FRA of 66 in 2018. Mike will reach his in 2020. Since she hasn't yet started collecting Social Security, they could time Melissa's claiming strategy to coincide with Mike's FRA, when she will be 68 and he 66. Or, she could wait until age 70 to claim her maximum benefit when Mike will be 68.

One other option is for Melissa to begin claiming her benefit now and continue to work. Since she's beyond her FRA, she can receive her full PIA plus some delayed retirement credits along with her full-time paycheck from the hospital. This would allow Mike to claim his spousal benefit now; however, as he's younger than his FRA, his benefit would be reduced.

Here's a look at how their benefits might work out (all numbers are approximate):

Melissa's age	Melissa's Social Security benefit	Mike's age	Mike's spousal benefit	Total household income from Social Security	Survivor spouse's benefit
66 (FRA)	$2,400	64	$1,010	$3,410	$2,400
67	$2,590	65	$1,100	$3,690	$2,590
68	$2,800	66 (FRA)	$1,200	$4,000	$2,800
69	$3,020	67	$1,200	$4,220	$3,020
70	$3,260	68	$1,200	$4,460	$3,260

Mike only gets his full 50% of Melissa's PIA when he claims at his FRA. Melissa will be 68 at that point. She could decide to retire and start her claim two years earlier than planned. She won't get the maximum from Social Security, but she still gets two years of delayed retirement credits, or about 16% more. Plus, Mike gets to claim his maximum spousal benefit two years earlier.

The other consideration here is how Melissa's claim affects the surviving spouse. While both are living, they get two paychecks from Social Security, but when the first spouse dies the lower check stops. The higher Melissa's check is, the more income stays in the household for the surviving spouse. Here is a case where getting more is better. Sometimes, more is just more. And that's a good thing.

It's just a little disappointing

Mike is so excited about this new-found income that he wants to claim right away. But that's not an option unless Melissa decides to claim now.

While it is fun to think about retiring and claiming right now, they know they needed time to work out all their numbers and develop a complete retirement income plan. It is just a little disappointing for Mike that they must work as a joint unit based on Melissa's record. Married couples where there is a non-wage-earning spouse must share a single working record.

Looking ahead

The good news is that Mike has new-found income in retirement. The catch is that the wage earner with the record must jump into the Social Security pool first.

There's more good news in that they don't have much longer to wait before Melissa will retire. Melissa is happy in her job. She can use these next few years to figure out what she'll do after the demands of her job end. No more 3:00 a.m. baby deliveries. No more emergency calls from new moms. No more 36-hour labors.

The decision about when and how to claim Social Security benefits is often as much about personal readiness and timing – and about spending more time together in the early golden years – as it is about the money.

Summary

Melissa and Mike are a married couple living in a "traditional" arrangement where there is one breadwinner and one at-home parent. In their case, though, the traditional roles were reversed. To Social Security, it does not matter who is the higher earner or who stayed at home. Of course, this arrangement was pretty much unthinkable back in the 1930s – a man staying home to raise the children and run the household. But, in the end, to Social Security it's just about the numbers.

11
She's Older And Already Claiming

Dwight and Amanda met when he started working in the same hospital where she had been employed for years. They were both divorced after short marriages (he had been married for six years in his 20s; she had been married for three years). They were quite "smitten" from the beginning, but they dated for four years. They wanted to make sure this marriage would work. Their concern was their age difference: she is nine years older than he is.

Married now for 20 years, they are doing just fine. He's 53 and she's 62. As a nurse in various surgical units and the emergency room for nearly 40 years, Amanda is exhausted. She wants to retire early, but they aren't sure that would be the best financial decision.

A pension and Social Security offers a way out

The hospital offers a pension. Amanda is eligible for $1,375 per month at age 62. She could get more if she waited until 65, but early retirement is her priority. In addition, the hospital is a covered employer, so she was on track for Social Security retirement benefits of about $1,000 per month at her Full Retirement Age (FRA) of 66 years and 6 months. If she retires at 62 and claims early Social Security, she would be eligible for a reduced benefit of $725 per month.

In total, she would bring in $2,100 per month as an early retiree. This was less than her current income, but with some trade-offs, like reining in some of their spending and cooking at home more frequently, they were both on board with her early retirement plans. However, they wanted to confirm one piece of information about her Social Security: When Dwight finally retires and claims his own Social Security benefit, will hers increase? And if so, by how much?

Dwight's Social Security situation is key

To answer that, we need to know Dwight's Social Security estimates. He worked on the technology side of hospital operations and had earned a good salary throughout his career. His last statement showed that he was on track for a $2,800 retirement benefit if he claims Social Security at his FRA. If he claimed at 62, the benefit amount would be reduced by 30% to $1,960. If he waited until 70 before claiming, he'd get a 24% increase in monthly income to $3,472. He is also entitled to a pension of about $2,500 if he waits until 65 to retire.

The clear focus for this couple, however, was their time together. Retirement is a balance between time and money. Some couples would prefer more leisure time together, even if that means some financial trade-offs.

If Dwight waits to retire until his mid-60s, Amanda would be in her mid-70s. If he waits to claim Social Security until age 70, Amanda will be 79. While they think they will live a nice long time in retirement, arthritis is already making it harder for Amanda to do some of the physical things she loves (especially gardening) and Dwight admits to being in better shape some 30 years ago. So, taking advantage of their early years in retirement is a top priority.

What happens to each of their retirement benefits depends on when Dwight retires and claims:

- If he retires at his FRA, he's 67 and Amanda 76. His Social Security income would be $2,800.

- If he retires and claims at 62, his reduced benefit would be just under $2,000 per month.

- If he retires and claims at 65, when his pension benefit reaches the maximum benefit payout, his Social Security monthly payment would be about $2,400.

Figuring out Amanda's spousal benefit

How will spousal benefits work when Amanda has also earned a benefit on her own work history? There are several steps to determining a spouse's benefit when there are two possibilities on the table:

- Amanda's maximum spousal benefit is 50% of Dwight's Primary Insurance Amount if she claims at her FRA. Half of Dwight's PIA is $1,400 per month.

- Amanda's own benefit is $1,000. If she claims at 62, she'll receive a permanently reduced amount of $725.

- She is eligible for a spousal "top-up" of $400. She won't be able to claim this spousal benefit until Dwight claims his benefit.

- Since Dwight is nine years younger, he must wait until he reaches 62 to claim. Therefore, Amanda is initially eligible to claim only her reduced personal benefit when she reaches age 62 and not her spousal benefit yet.

- Eventually, she'll get two payments: For the first nine years of her retirement, she'll receive $725 per month. When Dwight is eligible to claim, she'll also receive her spousal top-up of $400. In total, her Social Security benefit will be $1,125.

Whenever Dwight claims, whether at 62, 65, or 67, Amanda's top-up amount does not change. It is a calculated value based on Dwight's PIA, regardless of when he actually claims. But he must be claiming in order for her to claim her top-up.

That extra $400 in spousal top-up helps offset the 30% reduction in Dwight's monthly benefit if he claims as early as he can at 62. He would receive a payment that is about $800 less than it would be if he waits until his FRA. But, waiting those five years to claim means that Amanda has to wait until she is 76 before she gets any spousal top-up. By then, their years together may be fewer than they want.

Other options may be available

It may be that Amanda decides to retire at 62 but then decides after a year or so to look for some kind of part-time work. It could be in her nursing field, a supporting field, or at a garden shop. Any income on her part could impact the amount of Social Security benefits she's receiving (see discussion about the earnings limit in Part 3), but it may also help with some of the financial aspects of living in retirement.

Another option may be that Dwight can phase in to retirement. Perhaps there will be an opportunity at his current employer to work three days a week or in some other part-time arrangement. As a technology expert, he may also find other consulting or short-term opportunities. That might allow him to step off the full-time track earlier but wait to claim Social Security.

Summary

Couples with large age differences often look at their situation in two specific ways.

1. If time is the priority, the younger spouse might claim at 62, locking in a reduced benefit for their retirement but opening up the spousal top-up for the older spouse.

2. If money is the priority, couples with a large age difference should forgo early retirement and wait to claim until at least FRA.

Time, health, and wanting to enjoy the best years of retirement are major factors in most everyone's claiming decisions. The key to making good decisions is to look at your full retirement income plan and decide if and where you are willing to make other trade-offs.

Be creative in your thinking. There are many more opportunities for work in your 60s now than in previous eras. See what will work for you and your spouse.

SECTION B

Divorced women – the basics of divorce and claiming on your ex-spouse

12

Divorced Women – The Basics Of Claiming On Your Ex-Spouse

One of the biggest surprises with Social Security comes when divorced women learn that they can claim a benefit based on their ex-spouses' work records. The usual responses I hear are, "Are you kidding me?" and "Are you sure?" Here is one case where something sounds a little too good to be true. Coming at it with a healthy dose of skepticism is a good idea. But, no, I am not kidding, and yes, I am sure.

Many divorced women find out that their retirement won't be quite as dire as they thought because they will qualify for ex-spouse benefits on their exes' work histories. In the majority of cases, the ex-husband was the higher earner, so the divorced woman may get a higher monthly income.

Social Security recognized that spouses together formed an economic union, and as such, each spouse will be provided with a social safety net in retirement – even if that union didn't make it through the years. For much of 20th-century history, a woman's primary job was to stay home to care for the children. Even if she did work for wages, it was secondary to her husband's career and earning power. While this is not necessarily the case today, with many women working powerful jobs with significant salaries, it is the situation for many women entering retirement today.

Women's financial independence impacts the divorce numbers

Even in the 1920s and 1930s, as the Social Security Act was being drafted, the number of divorces was on the rise. This was partly due to population growth and more people getting married, but as women's economic independence expanded, more women also had the means to leave unhappy marriages.

The designers of Social Security did not initially address divorced spouses to ensure they too had a modest safety net of income in retirement. As the numbers of divorced women without their own work record rose over the years, their need for a retirement safety net became more urgent. In 1965, changes in Social Security provided for retirement benefits for divorced women who had been in long-term marriages.

In 1930, there were some 196,000 divorces. In 1960, nearly 400,000 divorces occurred. By 1980, about 1.2 million divorces were granted; another 1.2 million in 1990. The number of divorces has been dropping since the turn of the 21st century, but the sheer number of divorced women is high.[10]

Tens of millions of divorced women are living in retirement. Creating sufficient income to support themselves for 20 or 30 years is often a challenging road. That many divorced women can receive a Social Security benefit that is two or three times higher than what they could collect on their own record provides a real and sustainable difference to many.

Motherhood and divorce

Becoming a mother is one of the most important roles a woman can ever play. Frequently, women scale back successful careers to spend both quality and quantity time raising their children. The percentage of women who step off the career path for at least a few years to stay at home has remained relatively unchanged since the late 1980s. In fact, 28% of moms stayed home full-time in 1990, 29% in 2010, and 32% in 2018. The point when the fewest moms stayed home occurred in the early 2000s – about 23% of moms were home.[11]

---

10   Centers for Disease Control, CDC.gov
11   Pew Research Center, Sept. 2018; BLS, Employment Characteristics of Families – 2018.

So, what happens after you've stepped off the career track and years later end up divorced? Neither party wins financially in a divorce, but mothers are disproportionately harmed. They've severely reduced their work histories, and many will reenter the work force with significantly lower earning power. Almost all (98%) divorced individuals who receive alimony are women, but the amount they receive usually falls far short of the earning power they would have had if they stayed on a career track. The cycle of moving in and out of work can have a financially damaging effect during work years and in retirement.

As noted earlier, women's Social Security payments are significantly lower than men's. This is seen acutely in the case of divorced women, especially if they ended up as single parents. So, it can be a great relief at retirement to find out that your benefit may be higher as an ex-spouse than it was on your own spotty earnings record.

But is there a catch?

Well, a little. Not every divorced woman will be eligible for a payment based on her ex. The first consideration is how long the marriage lasted. An "economic union" had to be established to be eligible to claim on an ex. Social Security defines this as being married for 10 years or longer, consecutively. And there is no rounding up.

If you were married for 9 years and 10 months, that is not 10 years. You will not qualify for benefits on your ex. If you were married for 6 years, then divorced, then remarried the same person for another 8 years? Not 10 consecutive years. (The one small exception is if you were married, then divorced, then remarried within 12 months to the same person. Social Security will consider this situation as consecutive years. The two of you still needed to be married for at least 10 years, if you then divorce again, but the four- or five-month break you took won't count against you.)

Eligible ex-spouse benefits depend on a series of rules

If you meet the 10-year marriage rule, you may be eligible for a benefit on your ex's record. But there are other criteria that you must also meet:

- Each of you must reach age 62 before you can claim an ex-spouse benefit. That's because no one can claim retirement benefits before age 62, so you must both reach this age for either of you to qualify.

- Your ex does not have to be claiming Social Security. Unlike with married couples, you do not have to wait for your ex to claim themselves.

- If you are the younger spouse, you'll be able to claim as early as 62, since your ex will already be 62 or older.

- If you are the older spouse, you have to wait until your ex's 62nd birthday before you can claim ex-spouse benefits. This usually isn't an issue if the exes have similar ages, but let's say you are seven years older. You turn 62 but your ex is only 55. You cannot file for or receive ex-spouse benefits since your younger ex isn't 62. You can still file on your own work record, but you have to wait patiently for quite some time before claiming benefits on your ex.

• Your divorce had to be finalized at least two years ago. In other words, you can't get a divorce and immediately start collecting benefits as an ex-spouse. There is a waiting period. The exception to this rule is if your ex is already collecting benefits. In that case, you can begin collecting right away, so long as you are at least 62.

• Last, but not least, you must be unmarried to collect as an ex-spouse. That may seem obvious, but it is a point of confusion for many divorced women. Let's say a woman had been married to her first husband for 15 years, then divorced. Several years later, she remarried and has been married to husband number two for eight years. When it comes time to claim, it can seem that she has a choice to make: either claim on her ex or claim on her current spouse – whichever situation gives her the larger amount of a benefit – but no, it doesn't work that way. You don't get to cherry-pick which person you claim on in this situation. You are married (and hopefully, happily married!) to husband number two, so your only claim is as a current spouse.

- If you end up divorcing spouse number two, well, that's a different story. In that case, you can claim on whichever ex's record gives you the higher benefit amount. Keep in mind, all the other rules also have to be in place (both exes have to be 62 or older, both divorces were at least two years ago, etc.).

How the ex-spouse claim works

Let me put a few fears to rest here and now. If you are divorced, your ex will never know if you claimed on their work record and are receiving an ex-spouse benefit. You do not ask for their permission. You don't have to talk to them or consult with them. This is strictly an arrangement between you and the Social Security Administration.

You'll most likely need to schedule a one-on-one, in-person meeting with your local Social Security office. Bring proof of the marriage and your divorce decree. The Social Security agent will run the calculations for you. They'll take a look at benefit amounts based on your own work record and on your ex's record. Since you cannot have access to your ex's work history, Social Security will take care of running the numbers and explaining how you'll get a benefit based on the options available to you. Whichever amount is higher is the one you will receive. Let's look at a couple of examples to see how ex-spouse benefits work.

Example 1: Amber and Andy

Amber and Andy were married for 18 years from 1980 to 1998. Today, each is 62, and the divorce was 20 years ago. Amber has not remarried and would like to know if she can get a higher retirement benefit based on Andy's work history. He was the higher wage earner in their married life, and she assumes he continued to work over the subsequent years.

From her Social Security statement, Amber sees that her benefit is estimated at $1,100 per month once she reaches her Full Retirement Age (FRA) of 66 years and 6 months. If she claims early, her benefit will be reduced by about 28% to $800 per month. It would be pretty challenging to meet her basic expenses in retirement on such a limited income.

She schedules a meeting with the Social Security office, and they pull up Andy's work record. He did continue to work and earned a healthy salary over the years. His Primary Insurance Amount (PIA) is estimated to be $2,800 per month. Amber's benefit based on her ex-spouse will be $1,400 per month if she waits until her FRA of 66 and 6 months – $300 more per month.

If she claims at any time before her FRA, this spousal benefit amount will be reduced. If she claims at 62, her ex-spouse benefit would be about $945, but it's still a higher amount than the reduced benefit she'd receive based on her own work history.

This is good news for Amber. Andy will have no idea that her claim will be based on his work record. Furthermore, nothing happens to Andy's monthly benefit. If he waits until his FRA to claim, he'll still get his $2,800 per month. There is no reduction or "loss of benefits" because his ex is claiming on his record.

Example 2: Betty and Brian

Betty and Brian were married in 1970 and the marriage lasted just over 10 years. Assuming all other requirements are met, Betty can be considered for a benefit on Brian's work history. She chose to continue on her professional career track, and her PIA is $2,200 per month. Brian's PIA is $2,400 per month.

In this case, Betty will not get any benefit on Brian's work history, since her own work and wage history is high. As an ex-spouse, Betty would be eligible for half of Brian's PIA, or $1,200 per month. Her own record of $2,200 per month is considerably higher, so after meeting with the Social Security folks, she'll find that she's earned her own higher benefit.

Do ex-spouse benefits seem fair?

To some, it seems odd that divorced women might get a higher retirement benefit based on an ex-spouse they were married to 30 years ago. They were young and just getting started, so neither might have been making considerable wages. Years later, the ex can get a larger benefit because she was once married to someone who had a successful career.

Although a marriage didn't make it through decades, there was still a significant investment at one point. The divorced woman deserves a level of dignity in retirement. Keep in mind that these benefits do not make anyone rich. Social Security is social insurance that helps keep our older citizens out of poverty. The contributions into the program already account for supporting both spouses in retirement. In other words, all of these considerations are baked into the math when determining insurance benefit values.

It's interesting to note that divorce benefits are not a one-way street. They are not exclusive benefits for an ex-wife. If the ex-wife is the higher earner, her ex-spouse can and should claim on her work record. The same rules apply to men as to women. While the original rule was written with the intent of protecting women who are divorced from men, it now allows the lower-earning spouse to receive retirement benefits regardless of gender.

Divorce decrees cannot shrink ex-spouse Social Security benefits

It is distressing to hear from divorced women who say that they "signed away their rights" to their spousal benefits during the divorce proceedings. Sadly, some attorneys think this is allowed and build a clause into a divorce agreement stating that the ex-wife cannot claim on her ex-spouse.

This simply is not allowed. If this language is in your divorce decree, it is neither right nor enforceable. Meet with Social Security and get your money!

Divorce rules apply to same-sex married couples

As same-sex married couples qualify for retirement spousal benefits, ex-spouse benefits also apply to them. If your marriage did not survive, you may still be eligible for retirement benefits on your ex-wife.

All the same rules apply as for opposite-sex couples: you must have been married for 10 consecutive years or longer, each of you must be 62 or older, you must not be remarried, and the divorce must have been final at least two years earlier or your ex is already claiming benefits.

You'll need to bring required documentation to your local Social Security office, where an agent will help you figure out on which record you will receive the highest benefit for which you are eligible.

Divorced women have many questions

In the chapters that follow in this section, you'll meet two remarkable women who are divorced and working hard to create income in retirement. They have a variety of questions that you may have wondered about as well. You'll find more information about avoiding divorce pitfalls and a checklist and action plan for claiming Social Security when you're divorced on my *Boomer Retirement Briefs* blog at https://boomerretirementbriefs.com.

Read on for the following stories:

- Patricia is registered nurse who is divorced and a single mom. She'd like to tap her Social Security benefit early.

- Debora is high-spirited and delightful. She was married for years, then divorced, and tickled to be able to claim on her ex.

13

Divorced And Working: Should I Claim At FRA To Help Pay The Bills?

Patricia is registered nurse. She and Peter were married for 30 years, then they divorced. Their adopted daughter is a junior in college. Patricia is turning 66 this year, likes her job, and has no specific plans for retirement. She was thinking it would be nice to do more travel and pay the last three semesters of college for her daughter. She thought that adding to her income by claiming Social Security now might be a good idea.

Patricia asked: "Is it true that I can take my Social Security benefit while working without a decrease in my benefit? That way I could get some extra money now."

This is an interesting situation for someone in Patricia's shoes. And, there are lots of layers to her personal situation and her question. Let's take a closer look.

Answering Patricia's initial question

Let me answer her direct question first: Is it true that you can claim Social Security while working? Yes, indeed you can.

Social Security has a specific definition for "retirement". You are deemed retired when you reach your Full Retirement Age (FRA). Whether you are working or not does not matter. If you continue to work, you can make any amount of income *and* collect your full Social Security benefits.

Patricia was born in 1952, so her FRA is the month she turns 66. She can work as much (or as little) as she wants. If she claims her Social Security benefit at that time, she'll receive her full benefit amount.

In her situation, it might be a good idea to bring some extra cash into her household every month. If she's eligible for say, $1,000, that would be a nice boost in income and will help her enjoy some of the things that are important to her.

But wait, there's more

However, that is not the end of the story. Patricia has three other critical considerations to work out before filing a claim:

First, as an ex-spouse, she may be eligible for a larger benefit payment on her ex-husband's record. Let's assume Peter has a Primary Insurance Amount (PIA) of $2,200 per month. Patricia's benefit as an ex-spouse would be $1,100 per month. That's more than her own benefit, so she should claim on Peter's record.

Second, she needs to be aware of, and plan for, the impact on her taxes. Social Security benefits are subject to ordinary income taxes. Depending how much Patricia earns from her job, some of her Social Security benefit may be taxed as ordinary income.

Third, she needs to consider the long-range impact of claiming at FRA. If she waits to claim until after her FRA, she'll get more income for her entire retirement. For every year she can wait after her FRA, up to age 70, she'll get an extra 8% per year. Even if she waits just one year, until 67, to claim, her monthly benefit would be 8% higher than her benefit at age 66. If she waits until 70, her benefit will increase 32%.

Her calculated benefit at FRA is $1,000. Waiting until 70 gives her additional income of $320 per month. That is a big difference, especially to someone who

WHAT'S THE DEAL WITH... SOCIAL SECURITY FOR WOMEN?

has to count on only her own resources to make and maintain a retirement paycheck.

And there's still more

Patricia's case is particularly complicated because she was born in 1952. She's grandfathered into the "Restricted Application" option. This was a loophole that allowed spouses who were eligible for both their own retirement benefit and a spousal benefit to claim early on one record, then switch to the other later. This included divorced spouses.

In Patricia's case, she could file a Restricted Application with her local Social Security office and receive half of her ex's calculated benefit between now and age 70. Looking at Patricia's situation:

- Peter's full benefit is $2,200 per month; her ex-spouse maximum benefit is $1,100.

- At her FRA, Patricia files a Restricted Application for spousal benefits only and she'll get $1,100 every month from age 66 to 70.

- At age 70, Patricia flips her application to her own appreciated benefit. Her FRA amount was $1,000 in our example. With a 32% increase in delayed retirement credits, her benefit by age 70 has grown to $1,320 per month.

So, she'll get more than her own PIA from the time she reaches her FRA through her entire retirement.

If you're thinking "Wow, this sounds too good to be true!" you would be right. You can see why this was a loophole in the law that needed to be closed. The intent of Social Security is to provide only a modest safety net for retirees. With this strategy, Patricia is getting four years of "bonus" money that she otherwise would not be eligible for, and her own benefit grows to the maximum possible when she'll reach age 70. Since her birthday falls into the phase-out group, though, she is completely within her right to use this strategy.

Summary

The question from Patricia about claiming Social Security benefits while working clearly illustrates how one seemingly innocent question about Social Security benefits can open up a can of worms. It illustrates how much complexity there is in the system, and how Social Security tries to accommodate personal life situations.

If you are divorced, you may have the same options that Patricia has. Keep in mind, you will receive only one benefit at a time, and it will be the highest for which you are eligible.

- You can claim your full Social Security benefit the month you reach your FRA even when you continue to work full- or part-time, earning any amount of money

- If you meet the rules for ex-spouses, you may qualify for ex-spouse benefits of 50% of your ex's full retirement benefit once you reach your FRA

- You can wait up until age 70 to claim your benefits, getting an additional 8% per year in delayed retirement credits

- If you were born before January 2, 1954, you are grandfathered into the Restricted Application option

Remember that any Social Security benefit you receive is counted as income. In the years you are working, it is more likely that some of your Social Security benefit will be subject to ordinary income tax.

14

Married For Years, Then Divorced – Delighted To Claim On Her Ex

Every now and again a woman makes a lasting impression because her outlook on life is so positive. Debora was 68 when I met her. She attended a Social Security presentation that I gave in California. Afterwards, she waited in line a long time to ask me a question about her situation.

She was married many years before getting a divorce. She started reading about Social Security and thought she read that she could claim a benefit on her ex-spouse's work record. That seemed a little unusual to her, so she attended the workshop. We chatted afterwards and I assured her that if his benefit was higher than hers, she could indeed claim on his record.

Furthermore, she fell into the age group where she could claim a Restricted Application at her current age of 68, then switch to her own maximum benefit when she turns 70. I suggested that she make an appointment with her local Social Security office to confirm her options and get her estimated benefits.

One year later...

The next year, I was invited back to California to once again give a workshop on Social Security. Much to my surprise, Debora was back. "You can never get enough information about Social Security," she commented. She had come back to the workshop to give me an update on her situation.

She did indeed visit her local Social Security office after the first workshop. They ran the numbers for her about her claiming options. Since she was beyond her Full Retirement Age (FRA), she could either:

- Get her full benefit with two years of delayed retirement credits if she claimed then

or

- Claim on her ex's record – it was true!

Debora and the Social Security agent had an interesting conversation. There was quite a gap between

Debora's and her ex-husband's earnings histories: his Primary Insurance Amount (PIA) was about $2,000 and hers about $1,200 per month. They had two daughters together and Debora spent many years at home raising their girls. That left big holes in her earnings record. She mentioned that her first job was in 1965 when she was working for minimum wage of $1.25 an hour. So, many of her working years contained pretty low wages.

Decisions to be made and a challenge at the Social Security office

In her case, at age 68, Debora had a decision to make. She was eligible to claim her spousal amount of $1,000 per month from her ex's record or she could jump into claiming her own benefit, which had increased 16% in the two years since her FRA to $1,400 per month. Because she would get an additional $400 in benefits each month on her own record, the Social Security agent strongly encouraged her to take her own benefit.

But Debora was thinking long term and did not want to tap her own benefit yet. She was adamant that she only wanted the spousal benefit of $1,000 at this time. She explained that she was still working and that she wanted to wait until she reached 70 before claiming her own benefit. The agent couldn't get past the fact that Debora was "giving up" all that money per month. Debora had her plan, dug in her heels, and insisted on the spousal benefit. The first $1,000 check arrived the next month.

Claiming on your ex is a private matter

One of the things Debora told me when she returned for the second workshop was that she heard me loud and clear when I said that ex-wives do not have to discuss their Social Security claiming options with their ex-spouses. They don't ask permission from their ex; they don't discuss their plans in advance. The claiming decision is strictly between Social Security and the individual divorced person.

Well, Debora informed me that she picked up the phone as soon as she got home from the Social Security office and called her ex-husband! She reported gleefully that she just started getting a Social Security payment based on his work history. She could not have been more delighted to let him know, although she asked him why he didn't make more while he was working so she could have had an even higher benefit. Debora is clearly a woman in charge and one with a great sense of humor.

She also shared with her ex that she's using that newfound $1,000 per month to buy a new car that she really needed. It's a Subaru.

Her ex remarried sometime after their divorce, so he is not able to claim on Debora's work record. He also claimed his own benefit early, so his payments have been reduced. Debora was feeling very satisfied with how all of this was working out.

Social Security payments doubled

Then, something else happened. Debora turned 70 and, all of a sudden, she was getting a benefit payment of nearly $2,100 per month – double what she had previously been getting. Why?

She received several notices from Social Security. The first letter came a month or two before she turned 70 letting her know that her calculated benefit based on her own work record, plus the "bonus amount" due to her waiting until 70 to claim on her own record, was going to be $2,100. This was much higher than her initial PIA of $1,200. In fact, it is 75% higher!

The delayed retirement credits would have boosted Debora's monthly income by 32%. What she had not factored in was the impact on her calculated benefit of her continued work and the annual cost-of-living adjustments. She continued to work full-time all through her 60s and was even working the year she turned 70. Those earnings are significant and considerably higher than minimum wage. For each year where she had real earnings, a zero was replaced on her work record with real dollars. Since reaching her FRA, she's booked five more years of earnings on her Social Security record. And, if she continues to work another couple of years, even at a reduced schedule, those real dollars will replace more zeroes on her record.

The power of this combination can't be beat. Debora will just about double her monthly paycheck from Social Security by both waiting until 70 *and* continuing to work at a healthy clip so that more zeroes are replaced with significant earnings. Replacing many zeroes and low-earning years with higher wages can make a huge difference.

Is it time to retire?

Debora is trying to decide what to do for retirement now. She has her own small guest house at one of her daughters' homes, so she does not need to worry about housing costs in retirement. And she's worked long enough at her employer to receive a private pension.

She has five amazing grandchildren, ranging in ages from 3 to 17. She would very much like to spend more time with these treasures. And she is anxious to travel around the US in her new car, funded by her ex-spouse benefits.

Debora may want to do some part-time work, or she may be ready to fully retire. She's taking her time to weigh her options. And, while she's still working, she's still increasing her Social Security benefits. All in all, she's done an excellent job maximizing this very important source of income for her retirement years. She is simply delighted to have learned that she was entitled to a couple of extra years of income from those years she was married to her ex.

Summary

There were two critical steps that Debora took when figuring out her Social Security options:

- She started researching her options well before reaching her FRA

- She met with the Social Security Administration in person to get a look at her options

What was even more important was that Debora did not waiver on her plan of waiting until age 70 to claim on her own benefit. She had studied her numbers (available right on her statement) to see that she would get a larger benefit at 70 on her own record than she would get as an ex-spouse (half of his). She did not fall victim to the Social Security agent's strong recommendation of claiming her own benefit in the moment.

Like Debora, you may still be eligible for the Restricted Application. Your birthdate must be in 1953 or earlier, or on January 1st, 1954.

And remember, there is no need to let your ex know that you are claiming on their record – unless you just want to rub it in!

SECTION C

Surviving spouses – an overview

15
On Becoming A Widow

Much has been written about the dual dilemma of being a woman married to a man: We tend to live a lot longer than our husbands, yet our lifetime earnings tend to be lower. Before Social Security, a woman who was dependent on her husband for retirement benefits could be left with no income if he died first.

Social Security addressed the situation of widowhood early in the framing of the law. The lawmakers included a special set of provisions for a widow to continue to receive Social Security after her husband died.

Initially, men who became widowers were not afforded surviving spouse benefits. It took until the 1970s for Social Security to eliminate this gender bias. In one of Ruth Bader Ginsburg's signature arguments before the Supreme Court, she argued that a woman's earnings should be considered equal in their value to a man's earnings. And, thus, a widower raising his wife's children should be afforded survivor benefits.

Surviving spouse situations are complex

Thinking back to America in the 1930s–1970s, the country was thriving on manufacturing, coal mining, and industrials. It was an era where "heavy lifting" jobs were the norm. The odds of a male worker dying due to the job were high; thus, many widows were left to fend for themselves. Women became widows at early ages, when they were raising children, and in retirement.

The average life expectancy in the US in 1940 was 62 for a white male and 52 for a black male. By 1950, white males lived on average to 67, but black males only to 59.[12] Women lived about five years longer on average.

---

12 Data Sources: National Vital Statistics Reports, Vol. 50, No.6. *Life Expectancy at Birth, by Race and Sex, Selected Years 1929–98*; National Vital Statistics Reports, Vol. 49, No.12. *Deaths, Preliminary Data for 2000*; US Census Bureau.

So, how should Social Security address the situation of widowhood? What about the young mothers who were left to raise the children? Social Security retirement benefits were meant for retirement; but, if a husband died at 50, then what? Does a widow remain without any type of income for 15 years? It all depends.

The general provisions for widows

The lawmakers at the time looked at the situations surrounding widowhood and included provisions based first on the relative eligibility of the worker and then on the age of the widow. For example, if the worker was 65 or older and receiving retirement benefits, his widow would "step into his shoes" and receive that same amount, but only if she were of retirement age – 65 or older.

If she had not yet reached Full Retirement Age (FRA), she could get a reduced widow benefit as early as age 60.

What would happen to a younger woman who becomes a widow? What if she hadn't yet reached age 60? In this case, the assumption was made that she would have access to savings or life insurance, or that she would still be young enough to find work that would provide her with at least a basic income. She may have had to make serious trade-offs and wouldn't necessarily have been as comfortable as when her husband was alive.

These provisions and rules are still in place today.

Different rules for widows with children

There was one more situation that the lawmakers needed to address. Should survivor benefits be provided when a young woman who was raising the worker's children becomes a widow? The answer was yes. Social Security needed to be broad enough to deal with real situations that can happen to a worker's family.

In the case of a young mother becoming a widow, she would receive a surviving spouse benefit equal to 75% of her husband's eligible payment amount until their youngest child reached age 16. Furthermore, any minor children would also receive benefit payments of 75% of their father's eligible benefit amount until they reached age 18, or 19 and graduated from high school. If there are several children in the household, there will be an overall family maximum, so some adjustments to prorate payments may occur.

These family rules apply to all widows raising deceased workers' children. Sadly, some women experience widowhood at age 28 when their children are all under five years old. Sometimes a wife becomes a widow at 48 with three high schoolers. Social Security survivor benefits were written to address all of these situations. And widows have found this safety net to be incredibly helpful in a time of great personal and often great financial turmoil.

Funeral directors play a key role with Social Security

If you've never planned a funeral before, you might not know that the funeral director will ask for the deceased person's Social Security number. Why? It's the funeral director who immediately contacts Social Security to report the death of the individual and to relay any information about the presence of a surviving spouse and children.

As the death of a spouse can be a particularly difficult time, having someone inform Social Security that changes are needed can be incredibly helpful. Typically, someone from Social Security will contact the surviving wife and set new payments in motion. This helps keep the right amount of income coming to the widow, and it shuts off the deceased's payments.

If there is an overpayment, meaning that the deceased continued to receive payments after their death, it will be up to the widow to return the excess amounts.

WHAT'S THE DEAL WITH... SOCIAL SECURITY FOR WOMEN?

No one wants to deal with that on top of everything else going on in those first months after losing a spouse.

Special provisions for widows

Where the law acknowledges the plight of the widow is in allowing for earlier access to her spouse's retirement benefits. Instead of waiting until 62 to claim, a widow can claim survivor benefits as early as 60. Furthermore, her FRA is slightly younger as a widow than it is for her own retirement benefit.

And, maybe most importantly, the law set up survivor benefits in a separate tranche from regular retirement benefits. This allows a widow the maximum monthly payments at different ages, and it allows her to switch from one tranche to another if that gives her a higher payment.

Let's look at the options Sally Snowflake will have if she outlives Richard Raine. She was married to Richard but did not have her own work record. Assume she'll receive a full spousal benefit when she reaches her FRA. Also assume her husband claimed at his FRA and is receiving $1,000 per month.

Sally's Age	Her Spousal Benefit	Her Surviving Spouse Benefits	Considerations
60	N/A She's not yet 62, so she cannot access any retirement benefit	$715 She can access at a 28.5% reduction	No access to retirement benefits before age 62. Reduced surviving spouse benefits as early as age 60.
62	$350 A 30% reduction due to early claiming	$818 Reduced survivor benefits are available any time after reaching age 60 until FRA	At 62, Sally is now eligible to claim either her spousal benefits or her survivor benefits. Any claim before her FRA will be reduced.
66 (65 and 10 months is her surviving spouse FRA)	$500 Full 50% of his PIA	$1,000 She's eligible to step into his shoes and receive the full payment he was receiving	Now that Sally has reached her own FRA, she's reached the maximum amount of benefits she will be entitled to.
70	$500 Spousal benefits do not increase with delayed retirement credits	$1,000 Survivor benefits do not increase after the worker has died	There is no reason for Sally to wait until 70 to claim. Her maximum payments are available to her at her FRA.

What's important to take away here is that if you become a widow, regardless of your age, you have two "buckets" of Social Security income to consider. Whichever option gives you a larger check at that time is the one to go with. It's quite common to start claiming your spousal benefit at 62, receiving a reduced monthly spousal benefit, then switching to surviving spouse benefits at your Full Survivor Retirement Age.

What if a widow has her own work record?

If you have your own work record, you'll have three buckets to juggle to figure out when your highest monthly amount is available to you. It will be important to plan for this in your retirement income plan to ensure you know which strategy will deliver the most income for you.

Let's go back to Sally and Richard. Assume the same situation for Richard as in the previous example: his PIA is $1,000 per month; her spousal benefit is $500 per month. But now, let's say Sally also worked and her own benefit is $900 per month. What do her choices look like for claiming Social Security if she becomes a widow?

We already know that her own benefit is significantly higher than her spousal benefit ($900 versus $500), so she is not going to be eligible for a spousal benefit. Her Social Security will be based on her own work history.

Sally's Age	Her Own Benefit	Her Surviving Spouse Benefits	Considerations
60	N/A She's not yet 62, so she cannot access retirement benefits	$715 She can access at a 28.5% reduction	If Sally needed income, she could claim as a surviving spouse as early as age 60, at a reduced amount.
62	$675 A 25% reduction due to early claiming	$818 Reduced survivor benefits are available between age 60 and FRA	At 62, Sally is now eligible to claim either her own retirement benefits or her survivor benefits. They are reduced for early claiming.
66 (65 and 10 months is her surviving spouse FRA)	$900 Her full benefit amount	$1,000 At her survivor FRA, she's eligible to step into his shoes and receive the full payment he was receiving	Now that Sally has reached her own FRA, she's reached the maximum amount of her surviving spouse benefits. Her own benefit is lower than her survivor benefit, so she should choose the survivor benefit.
70	$1,188 Her own worker benefits increase 8% per year between FRA and age 70	$1,000 Survivor benefits do not increase after the worker dies	At age 70, Sally's own benefit has increased 32%. She can switch to her own benefit at 70, increasing her Social Security benefits.

For a woman in Sally's situation, where she has her own significant work record, it's generally a good idea to claim surviving spouse benefits at FRA or earlier, even though they will be reduced. This allows her own work benefit to increase to the maximum amount possible at age 70.

Household income falls for widows

It is critical for married women to plan for the possibility that they'll outlive their spouses. For couples where they are both already receiving Social Security retirement benefits, there will be a significant drop in household income when the first spouse dies. It is an unexpected, nasty surprise if you don't plan properly.

Social Security payments stop the month your spouse dies. That means if your husband dies on March 19th, his benefits stop effective that day. Both your payment and his February payment will be deposited in March since he was alive for the entire month of February.

Beginning with the April payment, you will begin receiving your survivor benefit. If your benefit amount was lower, you will now receive his larger amount as your monthly benefit. It is ⅓ to ½ less than what the two of you had been receiving. That can be quite a hit to your household finances.

Take a look at a few examples for Sally and Richard, who were both collecting benefits before he died. Regardless of how much Sally had been receiving as a spouse or on her own record, as soon as Richard dies, overall income to the household drops significantly – even if her survivor benefit turns out to be higher than her own benefit had been.

	Sally's benefit payment	Richard's benefit payment	Total household income from Social Security	% reduction after Richard's death
Both are alive	$1,000	$2,000	$3000	
After Richard's death	$2,000	n/a	$2000	-33%
Both are alive	$2,400	$2,000	$4,400	
After Richard's death	$2,400	n/a	$2,400	-45%
Both are alive	$1,800	$1,800	$3,600	
After Richard's death	$1,800	n/a	$1,800	-50%

It is critically important to remember this fact and to plan for this significant drop in income. The reality is when your spouse dies your household will not pay less in living expenses. In fact, it is rare that costs drop by much at all. The lights need to stay on and the taxes still need to get paid. So where will you make up for lost Social Security income?

Ex-wives can claim as survivors in many cases

Social Security addresses what happens to benefits for ex-wives. If you meet the eligibility rules as a qualifying ex-spouse (see Section B), you also meet the eligibility for survivor benefits. If you were married to your ex-spouse for 10 or more years before the divorce, you are generally eligible for surviving spouse benefits if they die first. If you can get a higher monthly check by stepping into your ex's shoes, you are entitled to the higher amount.

In this situation, it is unlikely that a funeral director will pass along the fact that the deceased has an ex-wife, so it will be up to you to contact Social Security when you learn that your ex has died. They will require that you bring in documentation to prove your marriage to your ex and the divorce decree. Then, they will take a look at all your options and help ensure that you get the highest possible monthly income.

For same-sex married couples, the same rules apply

If you become a widow when your wife or ex-wife dies, the same rules for stepping into her shoes apply. Since same-sex marriages were legalized at the Federal level in 2015, the same rights and benefits that apply to opposite-sex married couples apply to same-sex married couples.

When the first spouse dies, the surviving wife or surviving ex-wife is entitled to have her Social Security benefits reviewed and considered if there is a larger monthly payment available.

The same age rules also apply. If you were the wife who stayed home to raise the children, or your own Primary Insurance Amount is less than what you will receive as a spouse, you become eligible for spousal benefits on your wife's work record once you reach age 62. You become eligible for survivor spouse benefits once you reach age 60. And, if you are a young widow who is raising the children you had with your deceased wife, you and your children are entitled to family benefits. Your survivor benefits will be in place until your youngest child reaches age 16, but the child's benefits continue until they graduate from high school at age 18 or 19.

If you are unsure if any of the surviving spouse rules apply to you, call Social Security and check in with them.

Working and claiming can be dangerous

One area of Social Security survivor rules that surprises many is that you have to coordinate your work wages with your survivor benefits if you are younger than your FRA (more information on the earnings limit test in Part 3). If you become a widow and claim Social Security benefits while also working for a covered employer, you should expect a reduced amount in benefits until you reach your FRA.

The typical question I get goes something like this: "I'm a 58-year-old widow and heard that I can start getting survivor benefits at age 60. Is that correct?"

The answer depends on whether she is still working. She is generally still working since she's now on her own. When the answer is yes, I explain that while she can continue to work and claim her survivor benefits at 60, they will be reduced – and perhaps eliminated entirely – if she makes a good salary.

Keep in mind that survivor benefits are meant to provide income for a widow in her retirement years. Once a widow reaches her survivor FRA, Social Security considers her retired. In that case, she can work and claim her survivor benefits without any reduction. This strategy allows her own benefit to increase with delayed retirement credits. But, prior to FRA, any kind of benefits get clawed back if she earns too much money.

Surviving spouse benefits and remarriage

One last note about becoming a widow. In general, you qualify for survivor spouse benefits if you were married to your spouse for nine months. However, if your husband dies in an accident or while serving in the military, the nine-month rule is waived.

What if you became a young widow and later remarried? You are not eligible for surviving spouse benefits if you remarried before turning 60. However, if spouse number two dies before you, you once again become a surviving spouse. In this case, you will be eligible to step into the shoes of either spouse number one or spouse number two – whichever spouse had the higher benefit amount.

On the other hand, if a widow remarries after she turns 60, she can continue to claim her surviving spouse benefits until the time when she may receive more monthly income from her new spouse.

If you are thinking that all of these rules are rather complex, you'd be in good company. The only thing you really need to remember is that if you become a widow, contact Social Security. The agents will help you figure out which records you are eligible to claim on, and which one will result in the highest monthly payment going forward.

Take a lesson from women who have walked this path

In the following chapters, you'll meet two women who became widows at different points in time. You can download a checklist and action plan plus read about other women who became surviving spouses on my blog: https://boomerretirementbriefs.com. Read on to see how important Social Security is for women who became widows.

- Mary lost her first husband when her children were young. She later remarried and then divorced her second husband. After her second husband died, she got a step-up in income.

- Gail got it all right when she married her second husband. He was the love of her life. Eleven months into her retirement, he was diagnosed with cancer. Two months later she became a widow.

16

Married, Early Widowhood, Remarried, Divorced, Surviving Ex-Spouse

Marriage starts out so hopeful and we look forward to building a life and family with the partner we choose. Mary waited a long time to find the right guy. Donny was all that she could have hoped for. She was an older bride, so as soon as they said their "I do's", they started a family. Within three years they had two beautiful children. And life was good. Mary worked with children with disabilities. She loved her job but happily gave it up to stay home to raise her children. Donny worked for a large retail store. There were family picnics, vacations to the shore, and special time every night reading to the children.

And then the call came from the hospital that Donny had been in an accident and that Mary should come right away. He didn't make it. Mary went from her idyllic life to one of a widow with two young children quite literally in the blink of an eye. Her world fell apart.

Getting on new financial footing

There was a little bit of life insurance, enough to pay off the mortgage. Donny's army pension provided a small income. But it was Social Security that helped her keep food on the table in those first difficult years.

As the surviving spouse raising Donny's children, Mary was entitled to a survivor benefit before age 60. Each of the children also received a monthly benefit. They were four and two when Donny died, so their payments would continue for many years. Mary received 75% of Donny's calculated benefit at the time of his death. Each of the children also received 75% of his calculated benefit.

After the first year of adjusting to being a single parent, Mary knew it was time to get back to her career. She found a job working in a local school. This provided additional income for her and she worked "school hours" so she was home in the afternoons with her own children. But because she was working and earned more than the limit allowed for full payment of her survivor benefits, her benefits were reduced. The children's benefits were not impacted.

Getting remarried

Fast forward several years, and Mary met Nicholas. He was older by eight years, had lost his first wife several years back, and his children were grown and living on their own. They decided to marry. She was 50 and he 58. Since Mary remarried before age 60, her survivor benefits stopped, but the children's benefits continued until they each reached age 18.

Unfortunately, 12 years into the marriage, Mary and Nicholas decided to divorce. At this point, Mary was 62. She found herself eligible for benefits on one of three bases:

- Her own reduced Social Security retirement benefit based on her work history

- Her first husband Donny's record as a surviving spouse

- Her ex-husband Nicholas' record as a qualifying ex-spouse

Another new financial situation to set up

Mary was still working in the school district. She had some decisions to make about continuing to work and which benefit she should claim and when.

- If she claimed any benefit at 62, it would be reduced. In addition, depending on how much over the earnings limit she was, some of her benefits would be withheld.

- If she claimed either her own or her ex-spouse benefit, whichever was higher, she could switch at her Full Retirement Age (FRA) to her surviving spouse benefit if it were the highest benefit.

- She knew that Nicholas' benefit was the highest among the options, so if he died before she did she'd ultimately step into his shoes and get a higher benefit.

Her first decision was that she'd keep working. She enjoyed working with the children and wanted to keep busy during the day. Her income far exceeds the earnings limit on Social Security, so she would not request payments until her FRA.

A look at the many options available

Mary had three possible benefits eventually available to her:

Benefit	Mary's monthly benefit	Donny's calculated benefit	Nicholas' benefit
Primary Insurance Amount	$900 On her own work record	$750 Locked in when he died so early	$2,600 His PIA and the amount he was receiving
Spousal Benefit at FRA	$1,300 On Nicholas' history		
Survivor Benefit at FRA	$750 On Donny's history		
Survivor Benefit at FRA or later, if Nicholas dies before Mary	$2,600 Possible amount on Nicholas' history		
Mary's age 70 benefit amount from her own record	$1,188 After delayed retirement credits are applied		

Mary's goal was to get as much from Social Security as possible. Since she only had herself to rely on now for managing her retirement income, the decisions she made were critical to her future financial situation. After looking at the numbers, she planned the following:

- At FRA she'd claim her $1,300 ex-spouse benefit based on Nicholas' work record.

- Waiting until age 70 would not give Mary more income. Her own increased benefit of $1,188 is less than her ex-spousal benefit on Nicholas' record ($1,300).

- If Nicholas died first, she would step into his shoes and begin receiving $2,600 per month. And, in fact, this was the situation. At age 80, Mary heard that Nicholas had died. She met with Social Security and they switched her benefit from spousal to survivor based on her ex-husband's record.

Having a plan B is important when you're on your own

There was one other situation that Mary had planned for. She was concerned that she might lose her job before reaching her FRA. If that had happened, she would first have claimed her surviving spouse benefit on Donny. It would have been a reduced amount for a few years. Then she would have switched to her ex-spouse benefit of $1,300 at her own FRA. She had other savings and could have tightened her belt for a couple of years if needed. It would have been worth it to make sure she waited until her FRA to get her maximum benefit.

Summary

The rules around claiming benefits when you are a widow with young children can be incredibly complex. And, as long as you are eligible to claim on multiple people's records, you remain eligible all through your life. The highest benefit, among those you are eligible for, is the one you'll receive at the time of your claim.

It is easy to see how important Social Security has been for Mary and her children. It was truly a saving grace after Donny died so unexpectedly, leaving her alone with two young children. Unfortunately, her second marriage didn't last; but because it was a long-term marriage, it did open up another record that she could draw on when it came to retirement benefits.

17

Retirement Plans Cut Surprisingly And Unfairly Short

It takes years to plan the perfect retirement. And when you see it all coming together exactly as you had planned, the excitement builds. Gail and Bruce had been planning their retirement for years. They planned and plotted how they would spend their days by the pool, enjoying their growing brood of grandchildren, and sipping on a bourbon cocktail.

Gail was an executive at a large company for 25 years. When she announced her retirement, it was met with hearty congratulations. Gail's plan for retirement included working until her Full Retirement Age (FRA) so she could gracefully close her career chapter and joyfully begin her retirement years. Her financial plan was locked and she was ready for this new phase. Let the celebration begin!

It's party time

Gail and Bruce (who had retired several years earlier) kicked off "official retirement" with a road trip to Florida. Instead of wintering up north, they relocated for three months to southern Florida. Every morning they had coffee on the lanai, watching the surf roll in. For eight weeks, they entertained small groups of family and long-time friends.

Week nine was declared "party week". They invited 30 of their closest friends to join them in a weekend on the beach and a for special celebratory dinner at Gail's favorite five-star restaurant. It was quite a bash! And, for Gail and Bruce, it was the perfect way to mark this major milestone in their lives.

Sometimes, second time is the charm

For both of them, this was their second marriage. They each had two grown children and grandchildren from each of the four families. They took special care of each other, having come from first marriages that were not ideal. The love and respect between the two were evident in everything they did. It was a strong and powerful partnership.

Gail's first marriage lasted just over 10 years; Bruce's first marriage lasted 15. At the point of retirement, they had been together for 30 years, married for 25.

There was travel on the horizon and finally the time to do whatever they wanted to.

Retirement year one comes to a crushing close

Eleven months into Gail's retirement, Bruce was diagnosed with pancreatic cancer – inoperable, and the prognosis was not good. To say this was a shock does not even come close to what was going on in this family. It was utterly crushing.

They had one last Christmas together. The four children, their spouses, and all the grandchildren came together for a family celebration.

One year into Gail's retirement, the love of her life was gone. And her world stopped.

On becoming a widow

The shock of becoming a widow can push even the strongest, most capable woman to her knees. On every front there is something to deal with, all while the grief is overwhelming.

Fortunately, because Gail and Bruce had been planning for retirement for a long time, she was prepared financially. They did have seven weeks together at the end, allowing them to make final decisions about their finances, the house, and the children.

Social Security retirement benefits were relatively straightforward for Gail. She had claimed her own benefit a year earlier when she retired. It was a few months after reaching her FRA. Bruce had retired early and claimed his benefit, a couple of years before reaching his FRA.

They both had about the same Primary Insurance Amount based on their work histories. Their strategy was for Bruce to claim early and for Gail to claim at her FRA. Neither wanted to work until age 70 and they did not want to tap their hard-earned savings earlier than necessary. They each paid into Social Security for 50 years. It was time to take their benefits and use them as the foundation of their retirement income.

When Bruce died, his benefit check stopped entirely. His payment was less than Gail's, since he claimed before his FRA. Gail's payment continued to be deposited into her bank account, but her household income from Social Security dropped 40% when Bruce's check stopped. Social Security never missed a single payment, but it's still a jolt when one check stops. The funeral director took care of notifying Social Security that Bruce had died.

Was there another option?

At the point of retirement, Gail could have chosen a different option with her Social Security benefit. She could have used the Restricted Application to claim just her spousal benefit and then wait until age 70 before claiming her own benefit. That would have increased her monthly benefit 32% due to delayed retirement credits.

Or, if she had not yet been claiming when Bruce died, Gail could have immediately stepped into Bruce's shoes. She would have received the monthly amount he had been getting. When she turned 70, she could have requested to switch to her own benefit that would reach the maximum payout amount.

While these options sound good in theory, that would have meant that Gail would have pulled more income from her savings than she wanted to for four years. Retirement benefits from Social Security cannot be passed on to your children or grandchildren. It's your personal savings that are passed to the beneficiaries of your choice. One of Gail and Bruce's goals was to leave a legacy to the grandchildren if possible.

Deciding when to claim Social Security is about considering the various options and understanding the trade-offs. This makes it easier to put a good plan in place for your retirement finances.

Summary

There is no good time to become a widow. It's especially cruel to enter widowhood at the start of retirement, after working so hard all those years. To not even get a full year together, let alone five or 10 years, seems unthinkable.

Gail's advice to women entering retirement is to get your financial ducks in a row. Have a plan and understand where all your income is coming from. If your spouse dies first, one Social Security check stops. Know where you'll be making up that income. Know where the safety deposit key is. Know where every document is, where every dollar is.

Even as buttoned up as Gail and Bruce were, there were still things that fell through the cracks. She spent hours on the phone with a credit card company and switching the insurance policies. These tasks are daunting and exhausting on a good day. When you are grieving, these tasks seem insurmountable.

While it can seem unthinkable to plan for becoming a widow, the more you can do to prepare for the possibility, the less daunting it will be to deal with the financial realities if you become the surviving spouse. You'll need years to grieve and figure out what your new life will look like. Gail's advice is to allow yourself the time and space to get your legs back on solid ground. Having your financials in order makes this unwanted journey a little more secure.

SECTION D

Individual workers – defined as not married, not divorced, not widowed

18

What About All The Single Ladies?

When you think about the era when the Social Security Act was first passed, America looked very different than it does now. The country was relatively new in its industrial power. Family farms were still operating as family farms. Child labor laws were finally being enforced. We had come out of a world war, began manufacturing automobiles in droves, and finally began to recover from the crippling Great Depression. By 1935, when the Social Security Act passed, the country was slowly recovering, but many of our elderly continued to suffer in poverty.

Depending on a woman's economic and family situation, many worked outside the home. By the end of the depression, some 11 million women, or 25% of women ages 14 and older, were working for wages.

Huge numbers were working in factories making garments or candy or automobile parts. Some were school teachers, some nurses, some secretaries. Three out of 10 worked as domestic housekeepers or in personal service support. In farm country, women worked the family farms.[13]

Wages offered to women were substantially lower than those offered to men. Average annual pay for women in 1937 was $525 versus over $1,027 per year for men.[14] Women were often scoffed at for taking jobs outside the home. Society at large believed that for every job a woman took, a man was cheated out of a job. However, employers were happy to hire women at significantly lower salaries, and women were willing to take on jobs and low wages that most men would not accept.

Enter Social Security as a program for workers

With this economic and business reality as the nation's backdrop, FDR's administration came into power. One of the first major pieces of legislation enacted in his administration was Social Security. Central to this social insurance program was providing

---

13 US Census Bureau, 1930 census; Santa Rosa Junior College (SRJC) (2017) *Women in the 1930s and 1940s*. https://canvas.santarosa.edu/courses/24761/pages/women-in-the-1930s-and-1940s

14 Social Security Administration; SRJC (2017) *Women in the 1930s and 1940s*.

retirement benefits to workers when they reached old age (defined as age 65). It wasn't a program for male workers. Or white workers. It was simply intended to provide benefits to workers. That included the millions of women who were slogging through endless hours in factories, offices, and in other jobs provided by large covered employers.

Therefore, most paid, wage employment came with future retirement benefits for women. As they worked and earned covered wages, Social Security benefits were accrued, FICA taxes were withheld from their paychecks, and credits were earned. The fundamental difference, of course, was that women's wages were much lower than those of their male counterparts. Ultimately, their retirement benefits would be significantly lower. It's a problem that persists today. However, let's acknowledge that including women workers as recipients of Social Security from the beginning is nothing short of remarkable.

With progress on two fronts working in women's favor – the ability to get paid work and the prospect of receiving some sort of retirement benefit – women were now less dependent on men, and it was an option to remain unmarried. The 1930s were somewhat of a turning point in women's independence.

The single worker's benefit

Single women would receive a Social Security retirement benefit if they met the general rules:

- Earned 40 credits

- Worked for a covered employer

- Attained retirement age – originally 65, then later 62 for reduced benefits

The Primary Insurance Amount calculation is the same for all workers. The key for women is in defining exactly who is a single woman from Social Security's claiming perspective. This is one of the four categories Social Security considers for calculating benefits. An individual, or "single", worker is one who:

- Is not currently married

- Does not meet the definition of a qualifying divorced woman – in other words, was not married for 10 years or longer before a divorce

- Is not a widow

Single women become eligible for their Social Security as early as age 62. The penalty for early drawing is up to a 30% permanent decrease in monthly income. Without anyone else's work record to rely on, single women shoulder the full burden of the decisions here. And it might be well worthwhile for single women to consider whether waiting to claim until at least Full Retirement Age, or perhaps even until age 70, when monthly benefits are increased 24% or 32%, is the best strategy.

Solo responsibility for retirement

As of 2016, there were almost 59 million unmarried women in the US. About ⅔ have never married, and the other ⅓ are either divorced or widowed.[15] These women are single-handedly managing jobs, homes, and their financial futures. The vast majority will shoulder full responsibility for providing for their own retirement.

If you are single and do not qualify for any other Social Security benefit other than that of your own work record, one of your most important considerations is when to claim your Social Security retirement benefit. It will become a critical resource for income throughout your retirement.

There are many factors to consider when thinking about when to claim, including: how much you have in other retirement savings accounts, what your housing arrangement will be in retirement, how much debt you are servicing as you move into retirement, how

---

15 US Census Bureau (2017) *Facts for Features: Unmarried and Single Americans Week.* https://census.gov/content/dam/Census/newsroom/facts-for-features/2017/cb17-ff16.pdf

healthy you are, and what you will do with your time when you stop working. You do want to assess the importance of getting as much as you can from Social Security. The solid foundation Social Security will provide for your income in older age is simply too critical to leave to chance, and you must educate yourself about the implications of your decision.

Social Security decisions are top of mind for single women

It is impressive to talk with many single women. They are clearly knowledgeable about their retirement income options, and specifically about Social Security. They are thoughtful and deeply aware of their self-reliance. Unless they are faced with an external situation such as needing to care for an aging parent or unexpectedly losing a job, these single women are planning to work a long time, continue to save for their retirement, and enjoy all that friends and family offer.

Many single women are making specific provisions for their nieces and nephews who are important parts of their life. Others have found much fulfillment in volunteer work, and they plan to leave parts of their estates to the charities that are important to them. It is the level of involvement with their money that is so impressive. Married women could take a page or two out of the single lady's handbook and be very well served!

Meet two single women making great decisions about Social Security

In the chapters that follow in this section, you'll get to look into the lives of two single women who are owning their financial futures. Read about other single women and download your free action plan and checklist on my blog, *Boomer Retirement Briefs*, at https://boomerretirementbriefs.com.

- Jane – Married for nine years, she does not qualify for ex-spouse benefits. She's learned to make good decisions around working and her own retirement benefits.

- Karen – A single lady her entire life, she's built a successful career and a small business. She wouldn't trade a thing. Now that she's nearing retirement age, she's all business with her money.

19

Making It On Your Own, Even Though You Were Married

Jane remembers her wonderful childhood, growing up in the South, marching in her high school band, falling in love with and marrying her high school boyfriend. He was a free spirit and they wanted an outdoor life. They moved out West and started a family. They had five children (including two sets of twins) in short order, and she loved being an at-home mom in those years. Her husband never held a job for too long, did just enough odds and ends to provide the basics.

The marriage didn't survive. After five years, Jane knew things weren't going well, but they tried to hold it together. They were young and had responsibilities for their growing children. After eight years, they filed for divorce. It was final after their ninth anniversary.

WHAT'S THE DEAL WITH... SOCIAL SECURITY FOR WOMEN?

It was an amicable divorce, and the two remained friends over the years. They continued to live out West, jointly raising the children, and taking on odd jobs to keep food on the table. Jane loved growing her own vegetables and cooking with the kids. She found joy in the everyday things.

Time for a fresh start

After the kids were grown and launched, Jane moved back to her hometown. She's working hard to earn her own way. She's starting to put the pieces together to keep herself afloat financially and try to save something for the future. Jane has no regrets about her lifestyle from the early years, but she wished she had known the importance of earning enough to get to 40 credits for her Social Security benefits.

Now as she and her ex-husband are reaching age 65, it turns out that he doesn't qualify for Social Security on his own record. Jane hasn't earned enough for 40 quarters to qualify for her own benefit yet, but she is close. With her sporadic working history, where none of her years of earnings was substantial, or when she was paid in cash, her benefit amount is truly modest. She's working full-time now and is planning to work until her mid-70s if she can.

Qualifying on your own record

Jane was initially concerned that she would not be eligible for Social Security at all. She asked, "Is there any way to get Social Security when your husband never worked jobs long enough to earn his 40 quarters? A lot of his pay was 'under the table' and he didn't work for large companies."

It turns out that isn't even an issue for Jane. Because she and her ex were not married for the requisite 10 years or longer, neither of them can use each other's work record to claim ex-spouse benefits. The good news is Jane will qualify for Social Security retirement benefits on her own work record.

Jane is hardly alone when it comes to finding out her ex-husband does not qualify for Social Security – and that they weren't married long enough for her to claim on him anyway. Many divorced women only find out at the point of retirement that their ex-spouses aren't eligible for Social Security. Police officers, state government workers and some teachers have a pension instead of Social Security. Many women find themselves on the cusp of retirement with no social safety net.

Time to figure out your options

As Jane figured out, it's critical for her to get working and earning credits so she'll be eligible for at least a modest amount of Social Security. Jane wanted to confirm that she was on track to earn her 40 credits despite having a spotty work record. Fortunately, Social Security does not care when you've earned your credits; you just have to have a total of 40 to qualify.

Here at age 65, she has accumulated 36 credits. Just four more quarters to work and she will meet her eligibility to collect Social Security retirement benefits as an individual worker.

Jane looks much younger than her 65 years. She says she feels great and plans to keep working as long as possible. She doesn't earn a high hourly wage, so every dollar really counts. She'd like to find a new job with higher wages. Even getting an additional two or three dollars an hour will increase her wages enough to impact the highest 35 years of earnings that go into her benefit calculation.

It's a good plan for her to keep working as long as possible. Not only do these earnings boost her Social Security payments, but if she can wait until age 70 to claim she'll have earned all of her delayed retirement credits, increasing her monthly benefit check by 32%.

Illustrating Jane's possible outcomes

Social Security income will be very meaningful money to any woman in a situation like Jane's. It will be critical for her to do all that is possible to qualify for the benefit, and then to increase it by continuing to work in a job that pays a higher hourly wage.

- Her current Primary Insurance Amount (PIA) is estimated at $368 per month. If she keeps working and waits until 70 to claim, her benefit jumps to $735 per month.

- If she can find a job that pays an additional $3 an hour and work until 70, her monthly payment would jump to $779. That's more than double what she'd get if she retired at her Full Retirement Age (FRA) of 66.

When you have 25 years of zeroes on your work record, replacing even a few of those years does make a difference. Sometimes it makes a tremendous difference.

Does Jane's work after age 70 make a difference?

Absolutely. For many Baby Boomers, working after 70 is a real possibility and one that many are embracing. What happens to their Social Security benefits when they keep working? Do their benefits increase?

Yes, indeed they do, but not in the way you might be thinking.

When working for any covered employer, that employer is required to pay FICA taxes on your behalf – regardless of your age. Each year, Social Security recalculates your PIA if you have reported wages. So, Jane's PIA will continue to increase each year as she's replacing zeroes in her work history.

Even if she is working after age 70, she will want to begin collecting her Social Security retirement benefit by her 70th birthday because that's when the delayed retirement credits stop. She can only get 8% per year from her FRA of 66 until the month of her 70th birthday.

If Jane doesn't claim her benefit at 70, she effectively loses money. If she does not claim Social Security until she's 73, she'll lose three years of income. Social Security can only provide beneficiaries with six months of back benefits. Each year while continuing to work she'll get a new, higher benefit calculation due to her higher wages and cost-of-living adjustments. Jane can keep working until 90 if she wants, but she'll want to claim Social Security at 70.

Summary

Jane shared that it was a little hard to swallow that she has to create her own retirement after spending all those years as a wife and mother. But despite this, she's in great spirits, and moving back to her hometown, reconnecting with extended family and her friends from high school and finding a job that she likes was the right move for her. Overall, she's having a great time in her 60s.

When you are a single woman with a lot of gaps in your work record, there are important facts to keep in mind as you plan for your income from Social Security:

- You'll have to earn the 40 quarters on your own work record to qualify for retirement benefits.

- You'll have to rely solely on your own earnings to calculate the benefit. Social Security will use your highest 35 years of wages, including zeroes. The more zeroes you can knock off, the higher your monthly income will be.

- In a very few cases, you could be eligible for a minimum Social Security payment depending on the total number of years you had of covered employment.

- Your full retirement benefit becomes available the month of your FRA.

- If you can wait to claim until age 70, you'll get your maximum benefit that includes increases of 8% per year from "delayed retirement credits".

- Even after reaching age 70, you can continue to work. Your benefit will be recalculated every year.

20

A Life-Long Single Lady Who Wouldn't Change A Thing

Karen starts the conversation with, "65! I can't believe it! How did this happen to me?" Karen is a dynamo. A remarkable woman, full of life and energy and an unending supply of enthusiasm for last-minute adventures. She is a technology guru and website developer who's been running her own small business for 20-some-odd years. She loves her business and her clients love her. She's been an independent spirit as long as she can remember, and while she dated a little over the years, it was simply never important to her to get married or "settle down". She is staunchly independent and loves the life she's built as a single person.

With an Irish background, and sporting her characteristic red hair, Karen decided to study Spanish in college in the mid-1970s. She spent time in Spain, and her love of travel was born. Her career started as a high school Spanish teacher. While rewarding, it didn't pay particularly well. When a friend suggested she join a large computer company 1983, she made the leap. She got into the tech sector just as it was making its meteoric rise and she moved up in the organization in a variety of technology, operations, and project management roles. In 1997, the tech giant went bankrupt.

Karen was out of a job in her prime earnings years. Now what? She looked at her situation as an opportunity and decided to start her own business. What did she have to lose? For the past 22 years, it's been all good.

Along the way, Karen has stayed focused on a few key financial tactics. She is a self-professed non-financial person but is savvy enough to know that she owns her financial present and future. She bought a house within her budget decades ago and it is fully paid off. It was important to her to own that roof over her head outright, and well before she retired. Karen's been saving pennies, nickels and dimes over the years in various retirement accounts. That 401(k) that she contributed to back in her big-company days remains invested for her future. "Drive slow and steady" is her philosophy, so there's been no need for fancy, fast, or expensive cars.

Turning 65 and going strong

For her 65th birthday, she chose a long weekend in Las Vegas with a close friend. Her large circle of friends complained. They wanted to celebrate with a big party. Karen wasn't budging. "You aren't the boss of me! I'm going to Vegas my way for my birthday," she informed her friends. She watched the solar eclipse and was enchanted by Celine Dion at her Caesar's Palace concert.

While she didn't take her friends up on their birthday party idea, Karen has found that it's incredibly important for single women to have a close circle of friends and to listen to their experiences and insights. One of the most valuable pieces of information she's received from older friends is that Social Security income is not nearly enough. This is not something people often think about before they get ready to retire. Then you find out it's only designed to replace around 40% of your income for the average wage earner. It's not meant to cover all of your expenses in retirement, but when that first check comes in and you see how small it is, it's quite a shock.

Knowing that critical fact has directly impacted Karen's financial outlook. She has downloaded her Social Security statement and has been studying it. Assuming all goes well for her and her business, she's put a plan in place to work until age 71½. That was a pretty specific age. Was there a reason?

Confusion between Social Security's age 70 and the IRS's age 70½

For so many people whose expertise is not in tax law or accounting, it is so easy to mix up the seemingly crazy retirement rules. Karen had heard that 71½ was an important age – it's when she would maximize Social Security and have to take money out of her IRAs. Since her retirement income is solely on her shoulders, she would like to make sure she's getting every penny possible.

She was delighted to find out that her dates were off just a bit. She could, in fact, retire 18 months earlier than she thought. It was a good day when she discovered this! There is a lot of confusion around ages and dates, so let's clarify:

- For Social Security, your maximum payment happens the month you turn age 70. If you do not claim your benefit at 70, you may well leave some of your money on the table. Social Security will pay you a retroactive six-month lump sum when you claim, if you could have claimed six months earlier. If Karen waits until 71½ to make her first claim, she would have missed out on 12 months of income that was rightfully hers.

- Karen can continue to work well after 70 if she wants to. She would still claim her Social Security at 70. Each year thereafter when she continues to have income Social Security will take another look at her benefit calculation to see if she can get a larger benefit by including her current year's earnings.

- The IRS rules for retirement plans start at age 70½. This rule is called Required Minimum Distribution (RMD). The year you turn 70½ starts the clock. You'll need to withdraw a certain amount from any and all traditional IRAs, employer plan retirement accounts, and small business retirement accounts and pay income tax on that amount. There is a specific calculation used to figure out how much to take out of each account and report as income on your taxes. If you fail to meet the minimum distribution, you are subject to a 50% tax penalty.

- There is an exception to the RMD rule: If you continue to work for an employer after 70½, you do not have to take any amount out of your 401(k) or 403(b) at that place of employment until you retire, unless you are an owner of that company.

You can see that the rules are complicated and there are many places where you could go wrong. A small misunderstanding on Karen's part ended in good news. She won't leave any Social Security money on the table and she can retire a full year before she thought she could. She might not choose to, but realizing she had the option was unexpectedly good news for her.

The numbers are meaningful

Karen is planning very well and working hard to ensure that she has the maximum amount of income possible for her long retirement. She's pretty sure she'll have to stop traveling at some point, probably in her mid-80s, but she'll still need plenty of money to get her to 100.

Let's assume Karen's successful career started at age 22. At 65, she's got a robust work history of 43 years. She'll have 48 years of earnings if she works until age 70. When she looked at her Social Security statement, she saw four years of earnings were missing. She had zeroes from 1979–1982. Those were the years she was teaching. Instead of Social Security, her employer sponsored a pension plan. That was a surprise to Karen! She's wondering if she'll be entitled to any pension payment now that she's 65. She'll have to call the state teacher's union. Maybe she'll get a small amount if she met the minimum years for eligibility.

Otherwise, she's had a continuous and generally increasing work history. Her highest 35 years of earnings will be from her most recent years. With a strong income history, Karen's numbers might look like this:

- If she works until her Full Retirement Age of 66, her monthly amount, or Primary Insurance Amount, would be $2,032 per month.

- If she continues to work until age 70 before she claims, she'll get the 8%-per-year delayed retirement credit "bonus" and her monthly payments will increase permanently to about $2,880.

The bonus would give her more than $800 per month in additional guaranteed income – for her entire retirement. You can see what a powerful decision it is to wait to claim, especially when you only have your own income and resources to count on. If Karen can wait until 70, she will set herself up in the most financially secure way she can.

And the more Karen can pull in from Social Security, the less she'll have to tap her own savings accounts. That will give her more flexibility to travel whenever she wants, wherever she wants.

Summary

Women who have always been single tend to have a solid understanding of their financial picture. They are realistic about their capabilities and about the consequences of their decisions. Not all women are as adept at managing their finances as Karen has been, but their level of financial awareness is impressive.

Some single women will want to continue to work since it allows them to delay drawing income from their personal savings. Others want to retire early and pursue a new direction. The most important step is to take the time to look at all your personal resources and build a plan that you can get comfortable with. Keep in mind you may spend a long time in retirement.

Take the advice of the single women who have already claimed Social Security. The income is not as high as you'd like it to be, so choose your starting date wisely. It's all up to you.

SECTION E

WEP and GPO – when you have a state or union pension plan

21

Where There's A Public Pension, There Probably Isn't Social Security

What on earth are WEP (rhymes with "rep") and GPO? Teachers in 15 different states, those who work in their town or city offices, policewomen, and many others who worked for their state governments in some capacity know about WEP and GPO, and – let me assure you – no one is happy about these three-lettered rules.

Let's start with WEP, which stands for the Windfall Elimination Provision. This is a rule whereby if you receive certain types of public pension payments (those from your state or certain unions) as part of your retirement income, and you also earned enough credits to qualify for Social Security on your own work record, you will not receive the full Social Security estimate you see on your statement.

GPO stands for Government Pension Offset. This is a rule within the Social Security retirement program that affects your spousal benefit amount. GPO applies when you receive a pension from a job with a state or local government, the police, some teacher jobs or other positions, and you also qualify to receive a Social Security benefit as a spouse, ex-spouse, or surviving spouse. Your pension is meant to be your primary retirement benefit; consequently, your Social Security spousal payments will likely be drastically cut or even eliminated.

Some background

For decades, the Social Security Administration and Congress have known that Social Security was going to run into a rough patch due to demographic shifts. There would be many more Social Security recipients than workers to pay in to the program when the Baby Boomers retired. Many ideas were floated for how to help stabilize the imbalance.

One of the areas identified as a problem was a specific group of employers: the states and unions who choose to fund their own pensions rather than contribute to Social Security. These are the uncovered employers. The deal was that state workers would get a pension instead of Social Security.

If states opted out of Social Security, the idea was that the retirement benefits they provided should be fair. There would be no double-dipping of retirement benefits.

The WEP calculation

If you had a career in state government or teaching, and your only benefit is a pension, that is straightforward. At retirement, you'll get your pension benefit.

But what happens when your work history includes a combination of jobs where sometimes you're eligible for a state pension and at other times for a Social Security benefit? The rules here are that you'll get your full pension benefit paid in full, and your Social Security benefit will be recalculated to reflect an adjusted covered earnings history. In other words, you'll likely get a reduced Social Security benefit.

The reduction is calculated using a different Primary Insurance Amount formula. Social Security will take into account all the years when you earned a substantial amount of income from a covered employer. They will recalculate your benefit amount adjusting for the fact that you first and foremost have a pension.

There is a short paragraph on all Social Security statements that warns workers that if they have a state pension, the estimate shown is probably incorrect. But most people miss this little paragraph.

The GPO calculation

People also miss the sentence on their statement that says that if you receive a state pension, your spousal benefits will be reduced. Again, the coordination between teachers' unions or state pensions with Social Security exists to prevent people from getting two significant retirement benefits. If you are getting a sizable pension, you cannot also get a sizable spousal or survivor benefit.

Figuring out how much of your spousal benefit will be reduced due to your pension is straightforward. Take ⅔ of your monthly pension amount and subtract it from your Social Security spousal benefit, ex-spouse benefit, or surviving spouse benefit. In many cases, your spousal benefit will be reduced to $0. That is never good news for a you as a spouse, especially when you didn't realize that by working for, say, 40 years at your Town Hall, or putting in 35 years as a teacher in the 15 "special" pension states, that your benefit as a spouse would be greatly reduced or eliminated.

Again, the rationale here is that working for an employer that had a retirement system in place of Social Security does not entitle you to a retirement payment that is significantly greater than it would be if you had participated in the Social Security program.

A note about other pensions

In many cases, retirees can and do receive two retirement payments: their entire Social Security retirement benefit and their full pension payment. Why? How can that be fair?

Folks who worked in many large corporations had a defined benefit pension plan as part of their benefits packages. In addition, the employer was a covered employer, so their wages were subject to FICA.

It's not unfair in these situations – there are simply two distinct benefits because that's what the employer put into place. Decisions on designing and offering benefits packages are left in the hands of professional benefits managers. Each company decides whether to offer pension plans in addition to covered employment (so they fall under the FICA tax rules) or not. When payments were made into two plans, retirement benefits were paid to eligible employees from both plans.

Meet the women who will lose out on Social Security benefits

Many women find they will receive reduced benefits from Social Security based on their career choices and jobs from the last 40 or 50 years. While you can see how this seems unfair, their employers chose to provide retirement benefits using a different model – by providing a pension plan instead of Social Security.

There are many different situations that can occur with both WEP and GPO. Take a read through the next two chapters and meet the women who are dealing with planning for retirement income knowing that Social Security will not be a big part of their resources.

- Dianne's spousal benefits and survivor benefits will be impacted significantly due to GPO

- Susan's household income will be less than planned due to WEP and GPO

Additionally, go to https://boomerretirementbriefs. com for your free checklist and action plan, and to read about other women hit by WEP and GPO.

22

The Teacher With A Pension And The Corporate Executive

Dianne and Farrell are a long-time married couple. After 47 years together, three children, and nine grandchildren, they are happily retired and enjoying the time with family and friends. Looking back on their early years, they recall how Farrell traveled all over the country and to Canada building his career while Dianne was home raising the children. Her first career was as a nurse. She initially worked full-time and later switched to working on a per diem basis. The pay was good and she could arrange a more flexible schedule around the needs of her growing family. She earned her 40 Social Security credits as a nurse.

Her second career was teaching art. She always loved art, and since Farrell's career was advancing well, she was able to pursue a career nearer to her heart.

She worked for 15 years as a teacher, most of them in Massachusetts where the teachers participate in a union – not in Social Security. Dianne taught long enough to earn a pension, but it was not in the top bracket.

She and Farrell coordinated their careers and family duties from the beginning. They made key financial decisions together. There was a point early on in their marriage where Dianne could have been the bigger breadwinner, but instead they agreed that Farrell would pursue a corporate career while Dianne worked a more flexible arrangement and ran the household.

Complications in retirement

At 59, Farrell was retiring from corporate life, so Dianne decided to retire as well. They soon found that their life as a retired couple who needed to create their own paycheck got complicated. Farrell's career had been a straightforward one: he always worked for a covered employer and paid into Social Security. That wasn't the complicated part.

It was Dianne's career path that added some spice to the equation. It was typical for wives and moms of her era to be in and out of paid jobs – sometimes full-time, sometimes part-time, with some breaks in the career, and then a pivot in a new direction. From Social Security's perspective, Dianne was going to be eligible in two categories: as an individual earner and as a spouse. Two calculations were needed to see which benefit would give her the highest amount. (Remember that when you qualify in more than one category, Social Security pays you the highest single benefit, not both benefits.)

She had earned enough credits (40) during her nursing years to qualify for her own benefit, yet she only had 15 years of earnings. Her calculated benefit was modest. She would receive more as a spouse – 50% of Farrell's Primary Insurance Amount (PIA) at her Full Retirement Age.

The complication: Dianne also qualified for a state teacher's pension.

Dianne's retirement income situation

When Dianne applies for her Social Security benefit, she also has to report how much her teacher's pension will be and when those payments begin. As soon as that piece of the puzzle falls into place, Dianne becomes subject to WEP. And that means her modest Social Security payment is going to get more modest. She will indeed receive a Social Security payment, but it won't make her rich.

To understand Dianne's situation, the Social Security Administration will run a variety of calculations, including her reductions due to her pension.

- Assume Dianne's PIA was $700 per month

- Since she is also a spouse, her maximum spousal benefit is half of Farrell's PIA – let's say that would be $1,325 per month

If Dianne's career stopped after her nursing career, she would get the larger benefit of $1,325.

But she had a second career. And, because she was a teacher in Massachusetts, her pension will be her primary retirement income. So now, Dianne's situation changes to the following:

- Let's assume she'll receive a $1,500 per month pension from the State Teacher's Union.

- Her own Social Security payment will be reduced for WEP: she'll lose about half from her $700 monthly Social Security payment, netting her around $350 per month.

- Her spousal benefit will also be reduced due to GPO, so that $1,325 she thought would be available is reduced by ⅔ of her pension, or a $1,000 reduction. That leaves her with $325 per month.

You're probably thinking that Dianne is getting the short end of the stick here, but look at it through the eyes of Social Security. In an effort to create a fairer situation for all beneficiaries, they acknowledge that Dianne did pay into the system for the 15 years she worked. But if they use the standard formula, Dianne looks like a much lower-paid worker than she really was.

Her pension gets paid to her in full, plus she gets a share of her Social Security. Her total retirement monthly income is $1,500 + $350 = $1,850.

Compare that with what she would have received as a spouse ($1,325). By having that second career with a state pension, she actually receives $525 more per month than if she hadn't taken her particular path.

What happens if Dianne becomes the surviving spouse?

It's never pleasant to think about the fact that your husband may die before you do, but in the majority of marriages, that is the reality. If a surviving wife's Social Security benefits are less than her husband's, she would "step into his shoes" and receive the higher benefit.

If we assume Farrell's PIA is $2,650 per month, there are three options Farrell could take that impact Dianne's income if he dies first:

1. He could claim his Social Security at his FRA, receiving $2,650 per month. Dianne would "step into his shoes", receiving $2,650 per month if he dies first.

2. He could wait until age 70 before he claims his benefit. That would give him about $3,500 each month – a 32% increase in monthly income. Assuming they both live past 70, this is a great option. She'll get at least $3,500 as the surviving spouse.

3. Lastly, if needed, Farrell could have claimed as early as age 62. Remember that he retired early, so it could have been that they needed the income. His monthly Social Security benefit would have been just under $2,000 per month. If he dies first, Dianne would get at least $2,000 per month.

Not the end of the story

Now, let's go back to the fact that if Dianne becomes the surviving spouse, she'll continue to get her monthly pension of $1,500 per month. Therefore, when she becomes a widow, she is not entitled to Farrell's entire benefit amount. She'll step into his shoes, but they will be three sizes too big! The amount of surviving spouse benefits that Dianne will receive, regardless of when Farrell elected to start his benefit, will be reduced by $1,000 per month due to her pension and GPO. The outcome is:

- Her $1,500-per-month pension still gets paid to her.

- Her Social Security amount of $350 per month stops immediately.

- She'll receive the amount Farrell was getting from Social Security less ⅔ of her pension amount. Assuming Farrell claimed at his FRA, she'll receive $1,650 per month:

  $2,650 - [(⅔) x 1500] = $2,650 – [1000] = $1,650 per month

If Farrell could wait until age 70, Dianne would receive $3,500 - $1,000 = $2,500/month, but if he had decided to claim at his earliest age of 62, Dianne would only receive $2,000 - $1,000 = $1,000.

Coordinating benefits in a WEP/GPO situation is critical

It's always important for spouses to think about how their claiming decisions impact one another. It's extra important if you have a pension where Social Security retirement benefits will be reduced.

Farrell cannot make his claiming decision thinking about only his immediate income need. The decision he makes will live on much longer should he die first.

The decision would have been even more critical if Dianne's career path was one where she got an even larger pension. Let's say she was a career teacher whose pension was $5,000 per month. In that case, any spousal or surviving spouse benefits that she would have been eligible for would need to be reduced by ⅔ of her pension, or $3,333. In this case, regardless of when Farrell claimed his Social Security benefit, Dianne's benefit would have been reduced to as little as zero.

Summary

For teachers in the 15 states where your union provides a retirement benefit instead of participating in Social Security, it's important to plan early and consider the integration between the two systems. Your pension is paid to you in full and first. It is the primary driver of your retirement income.

If you also have enough years working for a covered employer to qualify for Social Security, your own benefit will be reduced. Any spousal benefit or ex-spouse benefit you are eligible for will be reduced by ⅔ of the amount of your pension. The higher your pension, the steeper the reduction.

Lastly, if you become the surviving spouse, your widow's benefit will also be offset by your government pension.

Planning well for all the scenarios when one spouse has a government or union pension cannot be overstated. It is critical to look at all the angles for when to claim, who should claim first, and how to think about the surviving spouse. Once your decisions are locked in, they remain locked in. Find a knowledgeable and skilled retirement income financial advisor to help you think about your personal situation.

23

The Professor And His Wife – So Much Math Involved

Susan and Paul met in high school, got married after college, and settled back in their home town. They have two children, almost grown and gone. They each started working in the 1980s, and their career paths have ebbed and flowed as opportunities sprung up and as they juggled the needs of their growing family.

Like so many of their generation, they moved in and out of jobs that held a host of different benefits for retirement. Now, on the cusp of deciding when to retire and what retirement might look like, they are facing a number of complicated decisions. Between the two of them, they have two pension plans, two sets of retirement savings, and two Social Security benefits to come. But there is nothing straightforward about their situation. The path each chooses will directly impact the outcome of income in retirement. Especially for Susan.

The path to retirement

Susan's first jobs were in corporate America, starting at an entry-level job, then moving up over the years. In the first 15 years, she worked for a variety of large firms. The last 18 years, she's been running a solo business as a marketing communications consultant.

Her first boss gave her great advice: "Just start saving in that 401(k) account. It should turn out to be a good savings account for retirement." She was 25 years old when she heeded that advice. Now, 30 years later, Susan has a tidy nest egg from her years of saving and investing in that 401(k), and she has a private pension that she'll be able to tap as early as age 55.

All of Susan's jobs were with covered employers. She's been paying into the Social Security system for decades. If she continues to work at about the same rate, she'll have a reasonably high retirement benefit from Social Security at her Full Retirement Age (FRA).

Her husband, Paul, "the Professor," had a very different career path as a math guru and engineer:

- For 18 years, he worked for a covered employer who paid into Social Security on Paul's behalf.

- For six years, he was an adjunct professor at a state university. The university sponsors a pension in lieu of Social Security; however, adjunct professors are not eligible for the pension. He had access to a small Optional Retirement Plan (ORP), but if he is invited to become a full professor any savings in the ORP get paid out in cash.

- In 2003, Paul was offered a full professorship in the state university system. He became eligible for the state pension plan. He'll meet eligibility at 55.

Nuances with pension plans matter

Being eligible for a pension is only part of the story. Paul's pension benefit will be determined based on the total number of years he's been employed in the system. For example, if he retires at 60, he'll have 21 years in the system. He'll receive 42% of his average highest three years of wages. If his average works out to $80,000, his pension payment would be $33,600 per year. If he continues to work until 65, he'd be eligible for the maximum payout of 50% of his highest three-year average, or about $40,000.

Those extra dollars could make a difference to their retirement income. Choosing Paul's retirement date will come with a financial impact. To boot, there is no inflation adjustment on the pension payment, so the final amount will be a lock.

In addition to teaching, Paul frequently gets tapped by the technical industry for short-term consulting gigs. He'll get a contract for a specified dollar amount and he's responsible for paying into Social Security on those payments.

As many educators find out, they have a true hybrid career. They often run into potholes with their Social Security benefits at retirement. Paul is going to be subject to both WEP (the Windfall Elimination Provision) – based on having both a covered work history and a state pension benefit – and GPO (Government Pension Offset) that will limit his ability to claim his spousal benefits on Susan's Social Security. The GPO also limits his surviving spouse benefits if he becomes the surviving spouse.

The first layer of complexity: Susan's income

There is nothing easy about assessing the best path to creating income in retirement for this couple. Each decision directly impacts another piece of their puzzle.

Let's first look at Susan's Social Security income potential. Assume her estimated benefit is $2,000 at her FRA. The small pension she has from her first job was from a private employer, so she is not subject to WEP. She'll receive both Social Security and pension income. If she wants to retire earlier than FRA and claim her benefit, she'll receive a reduced amount any time between 62 and 67.

Can a husband with a pension get a spousal benefit?

Knowing that Susan will become fully eligible for her Social Security, can Paul collect a spousal benefit on her record? If so, how much?

In a complicated series of steps, Paul will get to an answer:

- Paul's main retirement benefit is going to be from his state pension plan. Let's assume it will be $40,000 at age 65, or $3,333 per month.

- Paul also has a Social Security history, as he worked for a covered employer at the beginning of his career, plus several gig opportunities as a self-employed contractor. That's a total of 24 years of covered employment.

  - Because Paul has the state pension, his Social Security benefit will be reduced by a specific amount due to WEP: about $300.

  - Also, because Paul only has 24 years of earnings for Social Security to use in his calculation (short of the 35 years that SSA will use to calculate his benefit), he'll have 11 zeroes included in his calculation. Assume his PIA is estimated at $1,200 per month.

- When reduced for WEP, Paul can expect a $900 monthly payment beginning at his FRA.

• In total, Paul's retirement benefit is roughly $3,333 + $900 = $4,233 per month.

Now, back to Susan's benefit: to figure out if Paul can get a higher Social Security payment by claiming his spousal benefit, he'll have to apply the GPO formula. GPO reduces a spousal benefit by ⅔ of the pension amount.

• The maximum spousal benefit Paul could be eligible for is 50% of Susan's Primary Insurance Amount. Her PIA is $2,000, so his initial spousal benefit calculates to $1,000.

• Now, apply GPO: ⅔ of his $3,333 pension is $2,222. This is significantly higher than the $1,000 spousal benefit. Therefore, Paul is not entitled to any spousal benefit once he turns on his pension.

If Paul's pension were much smaller, it could work out that GPO does not completely eliminate the benefit. But, in his case, his pension benefit is large enough to wipe out any spousal benefit. He can, however, get a Social Security payment reduced by WEP on his own work record.

One more key consideration

Susan and Paul's planning for retirement doesn't stop here. They still need to plan for the fact that one of them will become the surviving spouse. Assuming Susan will become the surviving spouse, what will her income look like if Paul dies first?

- Since Paul's Social Security is lower than hers, Susan will keep her own $2,000 monthly Social Security.

- A key consideration is how Susan and Paul decide to claim his pension. The payment amount of $3,333 per month in our example applies if Paul takes the payout on his life only. It's the maximum pension amount he's eligible for. However, they need to consider the implications if he is the first to die:

  - If they decide on a single-life payout, they get more income while both are alive.

  - If Paul dies first, Susan will get $0.

One of the most difficult decisions couples have to make when pension plans are in play is whether to gamble on who will die first. If Paul dies first, Susan is left with no retirement income at all from Paul's working years. She'll keep her $2,000 per month (adjusted for cost of living each year) and her own pension, but her household's income will lose over $4,000 per month.

Where will she make up this tremendous income loss?

Looking at their situation from the other side of the coin: what happens if Paul is widowed? Can he get survivor benefits on Susan's record? In his case, the answer is no. Survivor benefits are also subject to GPO. Assuming Susan claims her $2,000 at FRA, Paul's pension is still too high to allow him any survivor benefits; ⅔ of his pension is $2,222, higher than Susan's benefit amount.

Paul would continue to receive whatever amount is coming from his pension plus his own Social Security.

When women face a significant income loss

Without a doubt, this is a difficult situation. Susan and Paul will either lock in lower pension payments so that they continue after Paul dies, or they will have to set aside other assets in the wings to cover Susan's income if Paul dies first.

It's also understandable that Susan and Paul are not thrilled about this situation. They both paid into the Social Security system when they worked for covered employment. Because Paul happened to find a great job that he loved at a state university, they are now looking at lower Social Security benefits – and, in fact, no spousal or survivor benefits for Paul.

The planning they do is critical. They will have to carefully weigh the pension payout decisions with a clear goal in mind to protect Susan.

One other thought from Paul: Now that he meets eligibility for his pension (at the 42% payout), what if he found another job at a large, covered employer? As an engineer with lots of skills and talent, he could find a new opportunity. His salary would probably be higher and he'd be adding current years of real earning to his Social Security record. Once he gets to 30 years of substantial earnings, the WEP reduction is eliminated. If he gets to a full 35 years of earnings history, his PIA could go up substantially. An interesting idea.

Summary

When married couples have complex retirement income situations, it can take some time to figure out the best strategy and the best timing for each person's benefits. Social Security calculations get extra challenging with WEP and GPO, and pension plans are even more difficult to get right.

Susan and Paul's situation illustrates how important it is for women to understand what could come their way in retirement, and how critical it is to closely coordinate with their spouses. The plans need to account for initial retirement income as well as sufficient income for the surviving spouse.

Retirement income decisions are big and important. They need to work in your 60s, 70s, and 80s – and, if you are lucky enough to reach 100, or beyond.

PART THREE
MORE SOCIAL SECURITY MUST-KNOWS

24

More For You To Think About When Planning For Social Security

So much of your final decision about Social Security will depend on your personal situation at the time of claiming. As you've read about these other women who are planning when to start Social Security based on their own situations, I hope you've been able to relate to one or more of them.

Before making your final decision about when to claim, there are other financial realities to carefully consider. Among them are the following:

1. **The earnings limit test** – This test is used when you are working but decide to claim Social Security before your Full Retirement Age (FRA).

2. **Taxes** – Depending on your overall income, some of your Social Security benefit will be part of your taxable income.

3. **Medicare** – This health insurance program is integrated into and coordinated with Social Security. There are implications to your benefit payment amount when you are both enrolled in Medicare and collecting Social Security.

Let's highlight a few key pieces of information on each of these topics so you have a basic understanding of them before you make your Social Security claiming decisions. It will be important to do further reading on Social Security's website and to consult with your retirement income financial advisor before making final decisions.

1. The earnings limit test

Many women are quite keen on the idea of claiming their Social Security benefit before they reach FRA. Recognizing that Social Security alone won't cover their expenses, they want to continue to work as well. That way, they'll continue to bring in their regular paycheck and get a boost in overall income by starting Social Security.

It's actually not a bad idea in theory. The problem for these women is that it won't work in real life.

The key piece of information you must keep in mind is that Social Security is a benefit meant for retirement. If you are still working, well then, you aren't retired!

Here's how the rule works

Anyone can claim their Social Security benefit as early as age 62. And, in fact, you can even hold down a job and get paid wages when you are claiming. But if your job pays you too much – the earnings limit – you will not be paid your entire Social Security amount. Any benefits over the limit will be withheld until your FRA and eventually paid to you over time.

Once you reach your FRA, you can work and claim Social Security. Then you'll receive your full benefit regardless of how much you earn.

An example

Let's say Sally Snowflake was born in September 1957. She's turning 62 in September 2019. She'd really like to reduce her work hours since she has a stressful job. She's thinking about moving to part-time and making up some of her lost wages by claiming Social Security.

Today, Sally's gross income is $55,000 working full-time. Her Primary Insurance Amount estimate is $1,616; she'd have to wait until her FRA of 66 and 6 months to receive that benefit amount. If she claims at 62, she's locking in a reduced amount and would receive about $1,170 per month.

Sally's income will drop to $35,000 if she goes part-time, and she thinks she'll make up most of it by claiming Social Security early: she'll get $14,060 for the year. Or will she?

Remember that Social Security is for retired workers, not those who are working part-time and want to supplement their wages. The definition of a retired worker in 2019 is someone who makes less than $17,640 in the year – the earnings limit. Sally's going to make about double the earnings limit; therefore, she'll have a benefit reduction. Since she will not reach her FRA this year (she is only 62), any Social Security benefits she claims will be reduced by $1 for every $2 she goes over the limit.

Her annual payment of $14,060 will be reduced by half of her excess earnings, or $8,680. The most she will receive in Social Security in the years before reaching her FRA is $4,700. And keep in mind that Sally's already locking in the smallest amount of Social Security she is eligible for by claiming at 62.

Three last notes about the earnings limit

1. Sally doesn't lose her benefits. Social Security will recalculate those "lost months" when she reaches her FRA or when she retires, whichever comes first.

2. In 2024, Sally will reach her FRA of 66 and 6 months. That year, her benefits may be reduced, but this will depend on the amount she earns before March. The earnings test is more generous, recognizing that many people will be winding down their jobs just before their FRA.

3. Once Sally reaches her FRA in March 2024, she can continue to work, earning any amount, and will be paid an adjusted benefit amount for her previously withheld benefits with no further reductions.

2. Taxation of Social Security benefits

One woman told another woman during a flight to Florida that, "Once you start Social Security and live in retirement you don't pay taxes anymore." She sounded very authoritative and confident. She couldn't be more wrong.

Unless you have income that keeps you in the very lowest tax bracket, you will indeed pay taxes on any dollars considered income throughout retirement. Your Social Security benefits are considered income. But whether or not you will pay tax on them depends on your overall household financial picture.

Taxation of a tax

The general rule for determining the taxation of your Social Security benefits is that if your household "combined income" exceeds a certain amount, a portion of your Social Security benefits will be taxed.

Many people think it is unfair to tax a tax. You've already been taxed on your income while working and paid 6.2% of your wages into Social Security, so why are you getting taxed on this insurance benefit? In order to help shore up the Social Security program back in 1983, during the Reagan Administration, an amendment was passed to tax a portion of higher-income people's Social Security. Unfortunately, the limits for determining "high-income" were not indexed for inflation. Every year, more and more retirees fall into the tax ranges.

For single women who have a "combined income" of $34,000 or more, as much as 85% of your Social Security payments for the year will be considered income and taxed as ordinary income.

For women who are married, filing jointly, if you and your spouse have a combined income of $44,000, up to 85% of both of your Social Security payments for the year will be included on your IRS Form 1040 as income.

Figuring out combined income

For the purposes of Social Security and the IRS, your combined income is a simple calculation. Add together the following on a special worksheet found in IRS Publication 915:

- Your adjusted gross income from page 2 of the 1040

- Any otherwise-non-taxable income (like tax-free municipal bonds)

- Half of your Social Security income for the year

- Half of your spouse's Social Security income, if you are Married, Filing Jointly

The sum of these amounts is your combined income. From there, you follow the steps in the worksheet, comparing your combined income to the upper and lower thresholds that determine whether some of your Social Security gets taxed.

The bottom line here is: if you've been a good saver and have IRAs and other tax-deferred retirement savings plans, or if you plan to work at all in retirement, or if you have a substantial part of your investments in non-taxable assets, it's going to be easy for you to exceed the combined income limits and your Social Security payments will be subject to income tax.

You or your tax preparer will need to run this analysis every year. Some years you might owe tax, some years you might not. It depends on your combined income each and every year.

3. Medicare and Social Security: Kissin' cousins

Another important factor to consider before claiming your Social Security benefit is how much your Medicare Part B premiums will be. Medicare is not free, much to many women's dismay. There are multiple parts, each with their own rules and costs. For the purpose of Social Security, it's Medicare Part B that we'll focus on. Here's why:

The Social Security and Medicare programs are knitted together. Once you are enrolled in both programs, they work together. The Social Security Administration is responsible for collecting Part B premiums. It does so by automatically deducting your premiums from your Social Security benefits before you ever receive your Social Security payment. It's not a choice. You don't opt in or out. It simply happens automatically. You can think of it this way: you'll never miss a premium payment to Medicare!

The result, however, is a big surprise to many women. They don't get as much in their Social Security check as they thought they would.

What is Medicare Part B?

Medicare Part B is the part of Medicare that helps you pay for your doctors and outpatient procedures once you reach age 65. There is an extremely long list of items that are included under Part B. Ask your physician and use the tools on www.medicare.gov to find out whether a particular procedure is covered under Medicare or not.

The best way to think about Part B is that it covers services and supplies that are medically necessary to treat your specific health conditions, and it covers many preventative services. There are still co-pays and deductibles that you may be responsible for, but generally Part B covers about 80% of the bill for covered services. That's why you pay a monthly premium – for the 80% share of the covered costs.

Part B premiums in 2019

The amount you will pay for your Part B premiums depends on your overall household income. The standard monthly premium in 2019 is $135.50 per month, or $1,626 for the entire year. That is a per-person cost, meaning that you'll pay $135.50 and, if you are married, your spouse will pay an additional $135.50. Keep in mind that the monthly premium costs typically increase each year, so check www.medicare.gov for updated premium costs every year.

If you happen to have high household income, you'll likely pay a lot more for Part B. Depending on your household's modified adjusted gross income, your premiums will range from about $190 per month per person to over $460 per month per person (for 2019; expect prices to be higher every year after 2019).

What to do about Medicare?

Medicare is an incredibly important and complicated program. It's going to be up to you to learn all you can about how you will get your health insurance during your retirement years – and to plan for the costs that you'll be incurring throughout retirement.

The best advice I have for you regarding Medicare and the premiums that you'll be paying is: spend some time on the Medicare website, www.medicare. gov. It is chock-full of information that you will need to understand before enrolling. Take the time now to start exploring how you'll get your health insurance in retirement and how much it costs.

When it comes time to enroll in Medicare, you'll sign up for it on Social Security's website (not on Medicare's website). Make sure you have your *my* Social Security account and your MyMedicare account set up in advance. The process will go much smoother if you have the right pieces in place.

25
Final Thoughts

When you think about all the women you know, some are married, some divorced, some widowed, and some single. Some have spouses they like, others don't. Some have been married and divorced three times. Some were widowed at an early age, then remarried, then divorced, then were widowed again. Some even have a spouse in jail. Many women or their spouses are Green Card holders. Sometimes young mothers became widowed while young children were at home.

Bottom line: every woman's life is uniquely hers. When it comes to Social Security benefits, it's all about you and your specific situation. Social Security seems rather complicated, but this complexity is for the best reasons. It's about helping women retain some independence and dignity in retirement – and retirement can be an exceptionally long time for women.

Will you live till 80?

Of course, no one can know that for sure... unless you're already 80 or older! From a retirement planning perspective, the general rule of thumb is that you plan for the odds that you'll live beyond the average life expectancy. For single women who are alive and relatively healthy at 65, their average life expectancy is about age 90, and 25% of women will live to age 96.

Married women's odds are even longer. A wife has a 50-50 chance of living to 94 and a 25% chance of living to 98.[16] Any way you look at these ages, they indicate a long time in retirement.

If you live a long time in retirement, would you rather have more income from Social Security every month or less? A higher monthly income should be a good thing when you reach your 80s, 90s and even 100.

This is not to say that waiting until 70 is something all women should do before they claim their benefits. There are lots of good reasons not to wait, but claiming

---

16 Society of Actuaries longevity estimates

too early at 62 or 63 has very real long-term implications for both your monthly income later in retirement
and your personal savings that you'll be depleting,
perhaps faster than you would have wanted.

Claiming Social Security is a critical financial decision

It turns out that claiming Social Security is one of
the most important financial decisions you will ever
make. We don't tend to think of it that way but, in fact,
it is a critical component of our financial well-being as
we age and lose options for employment. So, how and
when we claim sets up our financial foundation in a
meaningful way.

No woman in her 80s or 90s is happy to be receiving
less income than she could have. Many simply did not
understand how much they were entitled to receive.
By age 60, most women are tired. They've had lots of
bumps and bruises along their life's path. They'd like
to stop working or change up what they are doing.
Grandchildren are a strong draw to step out of work
and into the role of granny or nana.

Feel free to make any of those life changes. Retire if
that's what you want. But keep that decision separate
and distinct from when you'll claim Social Security.
You are making two decisions here, and both will

have significant consequences for your retirement income.

Now you know

Now you know that you are making two of the most critical financial decisions you'll ever make. In your 60s, you'll be making the decision about whether to stop working *and* you'll be deciding about when to claim Social Security.

These decisions will have financial implications 25, 30 and 35 years into the future. That should give you some pause before you make either decision.

The final take-aways

Here are a baker's dozen take-aways that may help you stake your Social Security claim wisely and well:

1. Sign up for your statement at www.SSA.gov/ myaccount and set up your *my* Social Security account. Use your statement to make decisions about how long to work and how much your monthly income might be.

2. Know all your choices for claiming and recognize that they can change over time as you move from one claiming category to another.

3. Understand the importance of your Full Retirement Age (FRA). It is your anchor for determining your calculated benefit.

4. Try to wait until your FRA before you claim. You can retire earlier, but wait to claim if possible.

5. Waiting until age 70 is nice, but it works for very few. You will receive 8% per year in "bonus" money when you claim after your FRA and by age 70.

6. If you claim any benefit before your FRA, you lock in a permanent reduction to your monthly income. Claiming at 62 locks in a permanent reduction of 25%–30% for all your remaining years.

7. While you can work and claim Social Security, some or all of your reduced benefits will be withheld if you earn more than the earnings limit.

8. If you are married and have your own record, make sure you are getting your spousal top-up when hubby or wifey starts their claim, if eligible.

9. Make sure you will be protected with sufficient income if you become the surviving spouse.

10. Read, read, read. This stuff is hard to understand, and it's complicated at first – the language is unusual and the concepts are not intuitive.

11. Recognize that the SSA agents are trained to deliver very specific information at a very specific point in time. They cannot and do not provide strategies for your long-term financial success.

12. Find a financial advisor who is an expert on Social Security as well as building retirement income plans. It is likely not going to be the same advisor who helped you build your nest egg. Interview a new advisor and get your financial house in order for retirement.

13. When it's time to claim, you can usually do so on www.SSA.gov, although claiming survivor benefits needs to be done in person.

I hope you have found this information to be helpful as a starting point. Keep in mind, only the Social Security Administration can tell you your actual benefit amount. Every woman who retires will eventually find herself face to face with Social Security. Learning more now should help you make the best possible decisions for your financial future.

Here's wishing you a happy, healthy and most enjoyable retirement, and Social Security payments that provide you with a solid financial foundation.

Acknowledgments

My most sincere thank-yous go to:

The amazing women I've met around the country who have been surprised by the complexity of Social Security, but who are now taking the time to figure out the best strategies for claiming their own benefits.

My friends and family members who were willing to be interviewed for some of the stories in this book. Each had such interesting situations that represent many women.

Susan Chanley, Ellen Feinsand, and Polly Walker – three women who started out as business colleagues and ended up becoming some of my most trusted friends and confidants. Thank you for all your support, ideas, and shoulders over the past three decades. (But who's counting!)

Julie Perry. You are a gem of a friend. You are always on my side, no matter what kind of crazy thing I've come up with. And you throw yourself completely into my book ideas, which keeps me motivated and moving forward.

Lucy McCarraher, my new publisher. I was nervous when my previous publisher sold his US company to a London company. He left me in your very good hands. I've so enjoyed getting to work with you and your team, particularly my fantastic editor, Maya Berger; project editor, Kathleen Steeden; and cover designer, Jane Dixon-Smith. Thank you all for your support and encouragement all along the way.

Judy Tarpley. You were the one who asked me 15 years ago about claiming at 62 while still working. That was the question that sparked my deep interest in how and why Social Security works the way it does. You never know the power of one seemingly little question.

Gabby and Susan, the mom-and-daughter duo at the Local Yolk in Plymouth, Massachusetts. I spent countless mornings in your coffee shop working on the book. You always greeted me with a big hello, a warm smile, and a delicious homemade breakfast.

My wonderful daughters, Katie and Lindsay, who make me laugh. You send the silliest GIFs and texts and pictures of your crazy cats to keep every day light and fun. I am so proud of how you are embracing your financial futures in your 20s.

Last, but definitely not least, my wonderful husband, Dan. I most appreciate your willingness to be a sounding board for my ideas and that you even made a few dinners (under protest) as I focused on getting just one more chapter done. I love you best.

The Author

My career passion is all about retirement and how Baby Boomers are reinventing retirement. I believe that every financial decision is a retirement decision – not just the dollars you sock away in your retirement plan at work or an IRA. (By the way, you do have an IRA, right?)

I am a mother, wife, daughter, sister, aunt, and now a great-aunt. It is the time spent with my family I treasure most.

To date, I've made 15,000 dinners for my family. I'll have another 15,000 dinners to make in my retirement years. Hope I'm up to the challenge. I'm an occasional gardener, marching band fan and ancestor researcher.

In 2005, I started Mantell Retirement Consulting, Inc., a retirement business development, marketing, and education company supporting financial services companies, advisors, and their clients. I hold two professional designations: Retirement Management Advisor (RMA®) and National Social Security Advisor (NSSA®).

My first book *"What's the Deal with... Retirement Planning for Women"* is available on Amazon. My blog, *Boomer Retirement Briefs*, at https://boomer-retirementbriefs.com, is a fun look at how Baby Boomers are reshaping and redefining retirement. I invite you to send me your retirement ideas on the blog or on Twitter (@MarciaMantell) or Facebook (BoomerRetirementBriefs).

Made in the USA
Monee, IL
24 October 2020

45910434R00144